BEAT INFLATION NOW

Turn Inflation Risks into Inflation Opportunities

Dr. Wolfgang H. Hammes

Beat Inflation Now – Turn Inflation Risks into Opportunities

Published by Hammes Performance Improvement Group LLC

For information about permissions to reproduce selections of this book, please write to the publisher: Hammes Performance Improvement Group LLC (e-mail: info@hammesperformance.com)

For information about hiring the author for workshops or keynote speeches, please contact Hammes Performance Improvement Group LLC (e-mail: info@hammesperformance.com)

ISBN: 978-1-944614-04-1 (paperback)

To my parents, my wife Angela, and my children Claudia and Maximilian

PREFACE

In 2016, I published *The Return of High Inflation*, one of the first books warning of a global inflation crisis. Back then, almost all politicians, regulators, business leaders, and investors were preoccupied with the opposite risk: deflation. Few decision makers or economists had inflation risk on their radar screen. This proved to be a costly and consequential misjudgment.

Following the majority view has rarely been an effective strategy to escape financial and non-financial catastrophes. In fact, most so-called experts and authorities regularly fail to anticipate major risk events. Not only did these authorities fail to see the obvious inflation threat, they confidently upped the ante in their pursuit of ultra-loose and highly inflationary policies and strategies. Being cheered on for doing so by many economists and business executives made a bad situation worse. We were sleepwalking into disaster.

Those who read *The Return of High Inflation* did not fall into this trap. They understood what was going on and enjoyed a decisive advantage over those who ignored inflation risks. Even today, this book provides valuable insights into the mechanics and dynamics of inflation and presents unique tools, concepts, and case studies to help readers decipher and manage inflation risks.

My goal was to provide an analysis of the many different problems caused by excessive inflation. Therefore, I included a detailed discussion of social and political risks that accompany periods of high inflation. History suggests that political and social order and stability is threatened when inflation spirals out of control. Unfortunately, politicians today seem to ignore this threat, as have others previously.

Today, high inflation is a reality in most countries around the world. The scenario that I warned of in my book *The Return of High Inflation* has arrived. High inflation has inflicted great pain on the general public and is unlikely to go away soon. Although there may be temporary relief[1] and short periods of disinflation, eliminating inflation will take smart, decisive, and coordinated action by central bankers, politicians, business leaders, and society and will require global coordination and cooperation. In my view, we are far away from such conditions; in fact, we are moving further away from them. Therefore, expect the inflation problem to get worse before it gets better. It may take a decade to regain full control over rising prices.

As *The Return of High Inflation* turned out to be a prescient and accurate prediction of today's reality, many people have asked me to share my current thinking on inflation with a new book on the subject.

After some contemplation I decided against writing a new book on the inflation crisis and its likely development. It simply takes too much lead time to accomplish this task. On the day of its publication, such a book would be already outdated. Because economic and financial crises move fast and abruptly, a book cannot catch up with the dynamics of a crisis once it unfolds. It is simply the wrong medium for this task.[2]

This book, however, is different. It is neither a continuation of *The Return of High Inflation* nor an academic analysis of the inflation crisis. Instead, it is my attempt to provide information and guidance on how to manage inflation risks, challenges, and opportunities in our daily lives. It was written for people on Main Street to support them in their fight against inflation. Most economists not only fail to anticipate inflation crises, they also

---

[1] Inflation does not move in a straight line. It often follows a wave pattern. During the 1970s inflation crisis we observed three inflation peaks. The first two peaks were followed by short periods of falling inflation.

[2] I will release online tutorials for self-study on this topic.

fail to provide useful and practical support to the general public. Therefore, I felt a strong need for a practical guide on inflation management.

While there are countless articles and books discussing inflation in general terms, what is missing is a structured and easy to implement Beat Inflation program for the general public; specifically, a book that enables people to launch their own individual Beat Inflation strategy.

Beat Inflation Now seeks to fill this important gap in inflation literature. It presents a structured program with more than one hundred ideas. It also contains many tools, practical checklists, and historic case examples. The focus of this book is on practicality and easy implementation.

However, beating inflation is only one of the two victories the reader should accomplish. The second victory is to become more successful in life and to build a high level of crisis resilience. Resilient people often manage to turn crises into opportunities. I want my readers to reach this level of crisis resilience.

It is my observation that most people perform well below their actual success potential. Failing to exploit your full success potential makes you more vulnerable to any form of crisis. The good news is that you can change this. You can become more successful and more resilient to withstand future crises. Often, a few decisive and surgical changes in our thinking and behavior will lead to outsized increases of our performance and success.

However, these changes require discipline, energy, and the willingness to deviate from the traditional way we think, decide, and act. The problem is that many people feel more comfortable following their established routines, habits, ways of thinking, and decision making. We simply lack an impetus to make change a reality. The current crisis could provide the much-needed impetus to change our lives for the better. Therefore, we should view this inflation crisis as an opportunity that represents the starting point for a successful reinvention of yourself and a more successful future.

The Double Victory Beat Inflation Program introduced here seeks to achieve these two victories by providing a structured program to help you beat inflation and make you more successful and resilient.

The program consists of four core activities:

- Improve your cost management (chapter 6)
- Reduce your risk exposure (chapter 7)
- Increase your income (chapter 8)
- Increase your productivity (chapter 9)

Successful implementation should enable you to contain inflation risks. This is your first victory. Some readers may even turn inflation risks into inflation opportunities by increasing their income at a rate higher than cost inflation.

Pursuing these four activities will not only help you beat inflation, they will also make you more successful as you pursue the four key success factors in life: smart cost management, thoughtful risk management, high income growth (through smart professional strategies), and high productivity. This is your second victory. Therefore, you should keep the Double Victory Beat Inflation program in place even when inflation risks have subsided.

Wouldn't it be a phenomenal outcome if you turned this crisis into a unique opportunity and a powerful success enabler? It is possible. Many great success stories began in the midst of a severe crisis.

I close by wishing you all the best as you pursue the two victories of the Double Victory Beat Inflation program. I also would like to thank you for the purchase of this book. I am honored that you chose me as one of your guides for this important journey. Please feel free to share your feedback, experiences, and comments with me.

Dr. Wolfgang Hammes

December 2022, Boca Raton, Florida

TABLE OF CONTENTS

INTRODUCTION: TURNING INFLATION RISKS INTO AN OPPORTUNITY

This book has an ambitious goal. It not only seeks to help you eliminate inflation risks from your life, it also wants you to use the inflation crisis as an opportunity to reinvent yourself. In other words, we will seek to turn a severe risk into a lifetime opportunity.

To that end, I have created the Double Victory Beat Inflation (DVBI) program, which seeks to achieve two victories. First, we want to beat inflation. This is the short-term goal. The second, and long-term goal, is to use the four core activities of the DVBI program to lift our performance to much higher levels. We want to come out of this crisis more successful, fulfilled, and happier. We seek to improve our crisis resilience to face the future challenges life will present us.

The DVBI program consists of the following four core activities:

1. Reduce your spending
2. Reduce your risk exposure
3. Increase your overall income
4. Increase your productivity

The program is based on research of past inflation cycles. It combines lessons learned from the past with new developments and opportunities currently available. This synthesis of the past and the present creates a unique set of ideas that are practical and easy to implement.

Both victories are achievable, because these core activities work well for both objectives: to beat inflation and to achieve transformational change in your life.

Therefore, the DVBI program should be continued after inflation pressures have subsided. The goal is to fully unlock your personal success potential and to achieve long-lasting personal growth.

WHAT IS INFLATION

Inflation describes the process that leads to rising prices for goods and services. There are typically two measures the media focus on:

First, the consumer price index (CPI) is a measure of price increases affecting a country's consumers. Second, the producer price index (PPI) describes the price development of input factors (e.g., raw materials) used by companies. The latter is generally considered a leading indicator. Rising PPI numbers are expected to impact CPI numbers with a short time delay.

It is important to understand that both figures are averages that are obtained by complicated mathematical and statistical calculations. Because CPI figures try to mirror the average consumer, your personal inflation rate may deviate significantly from the CPI figure. For example, the year your child moves from a public high school to an expensive private college, your household spending will go up dramatically. Therefore, use CPI figures with caution. Try to calculate or estimate your own personal inflation rate. The latter gives you a better indication of your actual inflation gap.

HIGH INFLATION IS A CRISIS, BUT EACH CRISIS PRESENTS OPPORTUNITIES

I am not underestimating the magnitude of the inflation problem we are facing. At the time of writing this book, we have just seen the beginning of the crisis; in many countries the problems will get worse. In my book

The Return of High Inflation, published in 2016, I warned of a perfect inflation storm that could lead to outcomes worse than those experienced during the financial crisis of 2007-2008.

Back then, I was heavily criticized for my negative views. This happens when you are one of the first global experts warning of a new risk threat. When *The Return of High Inflation* was published, everybody was worried about the opposite risk: deflation. Reality has forcefully made clear that deflation fears were unjustified.

High inflation is a logical consequence of our past excessiveness. While our reliance on ultra-loose monetary policies, extended periods of fiscal overspending, and escalating indebtedness produced past economic growth, this growth was not sustainable. We borrowed from future generations to consume today. Central banks supported this excessiveness by implementing ultra-loose monetary policies. Ultra-low interest rates (in some countries, negative interest rates) not only supported the debt-based economy, they also encouraged reckless borrowing and overspending.

What is happening now has happened many times in world history: a clean-up of the mess we created. This clean-up will take time and will create pain, fear, and uncertainty. There will be recessions, company defaults, and higher unemployment. However, and this is the experience from history, it will eventually end. Most countries will recover from the inflation mess and will return to more prosperity going forward. The storm will subside, blue skies will reappear, and the sun will shine again. No country in history, to my knowledge, ever ceased to exist due to high inflation. All have weathered the storm and recovered.

The length of this period of catharsis or clean-up will depend greatly on how well each country's decision makers handle the crisis. During the 1970s inflation crisis, Germany was much less affected than the United States and the United Kingdom. Germany's decision makers pursued different policies than their counterparts in other countries. Germany's past of having suffered major political, social, and economic crises (including a crippling hyperinflation) had an impact on decision makers and the general public. I hope that today's decision makers study past inflation periods in general, and the 1970s inflation crisis in particular, to build the competence base that is required for proper decision making.

I am also a realist. In some countries, politicians and central bankers will intentionally or unintentionally refuse to learn from the past. They will repeat the same policy mistakes their counterparts committed in prior periods of high inflation. Those countries will pay a high price for these mistakes. Social and political destabilization may occur. Living conditions may deteriorate to a point that many citizens will choose to relocate to other countries. The inflation crisis will drag on for many years, possibly leading to additional risk events.

Again, the next few years may become tough and challenging. However, there is a lot you can do to significantly reduce the inflation pain to you and your family. But you should not stop there. The good news is that modern technology will help us in many cases to overcome inflation issues.

WARREN BUFFETT TURNED INFLATION INTO AN EXCEPTIONAL OPPORTUNITY

When I studied the 1970s inflation crisis, I searched for both good and bad practice examples. Often, I only found the latter. This taught me a lot about what not to do, but little about how to contain inflation risk and turn it into an opportunity.

Fortunately, I discovered one exceptional (perhaps one of very few) best practice example: Warren Buffett, CEO of Berkshire Hathaway. His understanding of inflation and how it works was remarkable. Not surprisingly, Berkshire Hathaway dramatically outperformed other companies in the S&P 500 index. Warren Buffett increased the book value of his company by over 900%. Accumulated inflation, the benchmark he needed to beat to offset inflation, was 130%. It was a superb outperformance.

Chart 1: Berkshire Hathaway's Performance During the 1970s Inflation Crisis

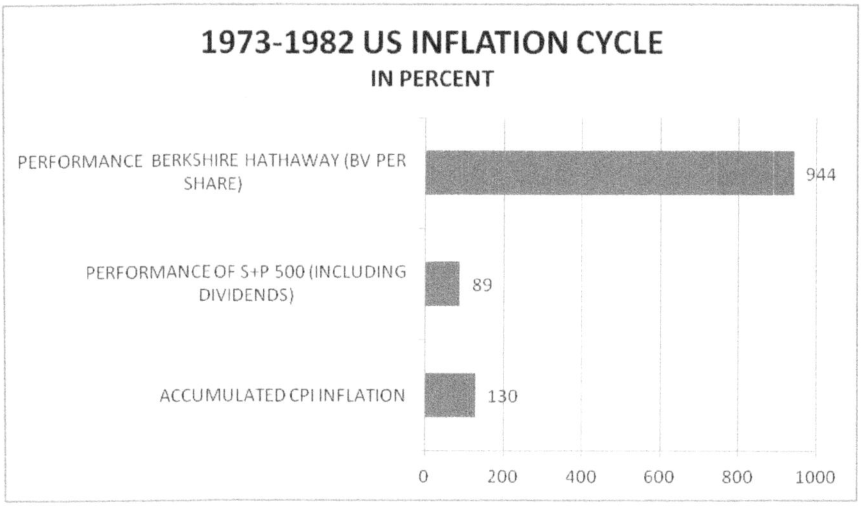

Warren Buffett adopted a dynamic strategy that constantly adjusted to changes in the macroeconomic environment (described by the Four Phases Inflation Management (FPIM) model that appears in *The Return of High Inflation).*[3] In short, Warren Buffett's inflation management knowledge enabled him to anticipate the macroeconomic changes that

[3] The Four Phases Inflation Management model is an important concept in inflation management. You find more information about the concept in the appendix of this book.

occur when an economy moves through the four phases of an inflation cycle.

Warren Buffett's experience shows that a deep understanding of inflation and proactive strategies will pay off. Obviously, not everybody will achieve such exceptional results, but it is an encouraging message.

UNDERSTANDING YOUR ENEMY: THE INFLATION GAP

We all face the same enemy during inflationary times: the inflation gap. The inflation gap describes the phenomenon that during periods of high inflation our cost-of-living expenses increase much faster than our income.[4] This leads to a deterioration of our standard of living as rising living expenses take an increasing portion of our income. If we do not initiate corrective action, the inflation gap will increase over time leading to financial hardship and the need to tap into our savings or credit products (e.g., loans, credit cards) to cover financial shortfalls (see Chart 2).

[4] Please note that you pay your expenses with income after taxes. Salary increases are partly consumed by higher income taxes. Inflation on the other side is a pre-tax expense (making your purchases more expensive).

Chart 2: The Inflation Gap

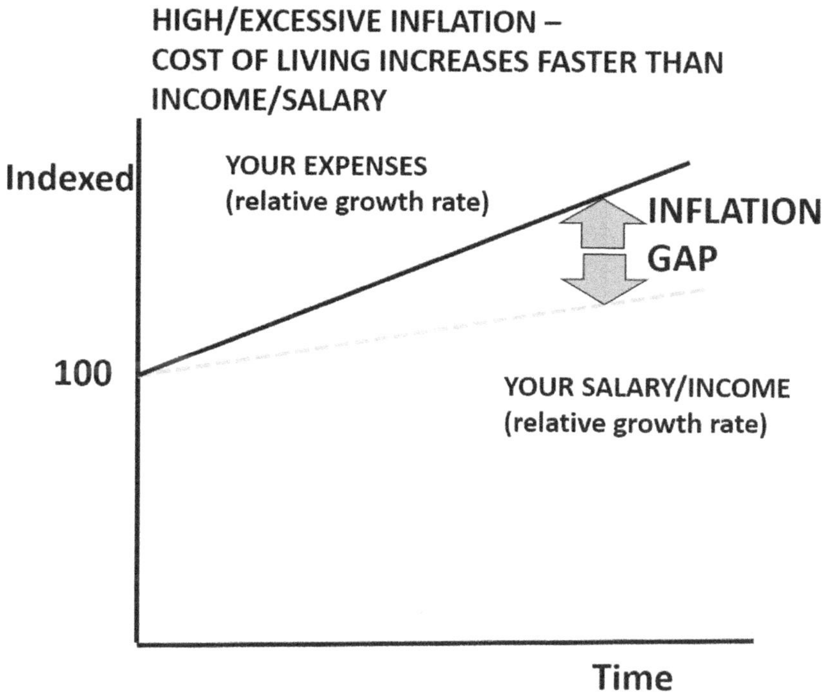

The good news is that you are reading this book (perhaps other inflation books as well) and understand the need for corrective action. This is the first and, probably, most important step. You are moving from inaction to action. Therefore, something positive is likely to happen due to your action.

The DVBI program will present many ideas and action steps to tackle your personal inflation problem. Some will be quite exciting as they have the potential to turn you into a more successful person than before. The goal of the DVBI program is to fully eliminate the inflation gap (see Chart 3); that is, to make your income grow faster than your expenses.

Chart 3: Eliminating the Inflation Gap

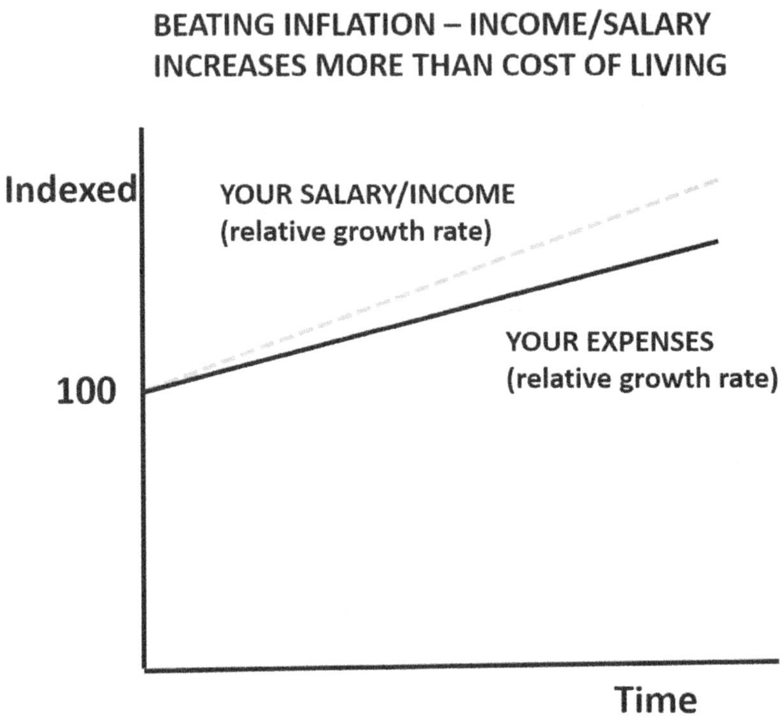

You may ask, how likely is it that you will achieve such a favorable outcome? The answer will greatly depend on you and your determination to achieve this objective. You will need to invest time and effort into the program, but I hope you will feel good about these investments. I also hope you will feel positive about reinventing yourself by changing your habits and thought patterns, which is necessary to achieve the improvements the DVBI program seeks to accomplish.

Keep in mind that at any point in time, we exploit only a fraction of our current success potential. All of us possess hidden skills, talents, and capabilities that we have not tapped into yet. Now is the time to access these hidden reserves and to monetize them. In addition, we can learn new skills, accumulate new experiences, or enter new professional arenas. All these activities can help make you more valuable in the professional world.

Finding new professional arenas is an important issue. An arena is the place you operate and compete in (i.e., your profession, geographical location, current employer). Most people take their current arena as a given. For example, working in a lowly paid administrative job in city ABC. But it is not. You can move to a new arena at any point in time. If you believe that a different arena (e.g., a different job) will provide better life outcomes you should consider making a change in your life. You are in the driver's seat. If a new direction is more promising, why stick with the old one? You will need such flexibility and strategic agility during periods of high inflation. Sometimes just taking one educational class can make a huge difference in the job market. It may allow you to move into a significantly more attractive arena.

THIS INFLATION PERIOD IS DIFFERENT, WITH MORE OPPORTUNITIES THAN DURING THE 1970s

I would not be as positive about the prospects of beating inflation if we were still stuck in 1970s' living conditions, with a rigid labor market, no internet, no price transparency, no video conferencing, and no smartphones.

Today, our world is different thanks to technology and the evolution of new business practices. One of the many differences is the "gig" economy. You can live on the West Coast of the United States and work on a project for a company on the East Coast. If you have a special skill, you can create an online course and market it globally. You can accept jobs creating additional income regardless of your location. You can write a book and sell it (without a publisher) around the world yourself thanks to new electronic platforms. Technology and the "gig" economy can become your secret weapons in the fight against inflation and in your pursuit to become more successful. The good news is: You do not have to be a technology wizard to use these opportunities.

THE DOUBLE VICTORY BEAT INFLATION PROGRAM

The DVBI program seeks to help you achieve two major victories in your life:

1. Beat inflation by closing the inflation gap (short- to mid-term).
2. Reinvent yourself and become a more successful, fulfilled, and happier person (long-term).

These goals are ambitious but they are attainable; therefore, we should not settle for less. They might be stretch goals, but the good thing about stretch goals is that they make us even prouder and happier once we accomplish them.

The program consists of four core activities:

Reducing your expenses is the first core activity and is the one that will have the most immediate impact. The dollar you did not spend is an extra dollar in your bank account earning interest (i.e., income) for as long as you do not spend it.

Spending less can be a liberating and success-improving activity, particularly if you reduce spending on items that lead to value-destructing distractions (e.g., computer games, streaming services), create short-lived pleasure, negatively impact your health (e.g., junk food), or are done to impress others.

The second core activity is concerned with our risk taking. High inflation is a high-risk event. Therefore, we should not take on additional risks that do not lead to sizeable opportunities. Remember, any risk you take can turn into an additional expense or a financial loss. Often, we think about risk management solely in the context of our investments. However, the topic is much wider than that. For example, living an unhealthy life will lead to higher health care spending in the future. In some countries, health care expenses rise even faster than official inflation rates. Therefore, living healthier is also an important inflation hedge that may save us a lot of money in the future.

In general, we should be cautious with any form of risk-taking during periods of high inflation. Only risks that come with outsized opportunities should be considered. All other risks should be avoided, at least until the inflation storm has passed.

The most exciting core activity is the third one: increase your income by using all opportunities available to you. This includes obtaining salary increases that match inflation rates as well as finding new ways to generate additional income. The latter has become much easier given technology-enabled opportunities (e.g., creating online classes, affiliate marketing) and the establishment of the gig economy that matches providers and buyers of services and products worldwide.

The last core activity seeks to improve your productivity, an important activity that is often overlooked. Highly successful people are typically also highly productive ones. High productivity not only means that you achieve more in less time (and thus can reinvest some time in the DBVI program), it also has a much bigger influence on your life. Supervisors notice productive employees, who are in short supply. It will not take long before you will be offered more job-related responsibilities and opportunities. Typically, this leads to promotion and attractive salary increases. Therefore, we will use the inflation crisis as a forcing device to increase our productivity.

The four core activities of the DVBI program work not only during inflationary times but in any type of environment. Therefore, I encourage you to continue the program past the point you have declared victory over inflation.

DO NOT BATTLE INFLATION ALONE – CREATE A BEAT INFLATION TEAM

The biggest mistake people make when facing a problem or a material risk is to address it alone. You can achieve a lot in life, but very little alone. Becoming a loner during times of crisis is a dangerous path to choose. Not only will you give up the enormous cross-fertilization that occurs when working in teams and exchanging views and ideas, you may also fall into an emotional hole when success is delayed with no one offering a hand to pull you out or to lift your spirits. Please do not do this.

I created the DVBI program as a team approach. While it is true that you can do most activities on your own, I recommend that you build your own Beat Inflation team. Ask friends, relatives, and colleagues to join you in your effort to create and implement strategies to beat inflation. The more diverse the team, the better. You need different perspectives, diverse educational backgrounds, new experiences, and new ways of thinking. By using videoconferencing and other technologies, you can create a remote team with members who live in different parts of the country or in different countries.

Meet once per week and exchange ideas, strategies, and experiences. Make plans for what to accomplish the next week. Let others help you when you face a problem and help others when they need support. It will be a win-win for everybody. You may even talk about entrepreneurial activities that you may pursue jointly. Wouldn't it be great if a large number of successful start-ups originate from these Beat Inflation teams?

THE ULTIMATE GOAL: BEAT INFLATION TEAMS EXCHANGE THEIR IDEAS AND PROVIDE MUTUAL SUPPORT

My vision for the DVBI initiative is that Beat Inflation teams will communicate with each other and exchange ideas, experiences, and strategies. Beating inflation is not a competition in which one team wins and the other one loses. All of us can win. The prize money is unlimited. Helping others does not reduce your success. Instead, a culture of sharing will probably help our respective countries to recover much faster from the inflation crisis.

COOPERATION AND TEAM SPIRIT

In 1993, I published my doctoral dissertation on the superiority of cooperation strategies over competition in the business world and society. I proved that the concept of cooperation and building strategic alliances is a powerful tool to become more successful.

This book builds on this important thought. Fighting inflation could become a turning point in the alarming and frightening trend of our societies to become more polarized and fragmented. Let us use the fight against inflation to reverse this dangerous trend and create societies that are open-minded, mutually supportive, cooperative, and tolerant of each other's views. It will be a better place for all of us.

HOW TO USE THIS BOOK

Let us go to work. The first part of the book discusses the current inflation situation. It is important that you understand the inflation problem in great detail, before you develop your Beat Inflation strategy.

The second part of the book is focused on fighting inflation and closing the inflation gap. Many activities and ideas are presented. It is important that you approach these ideas with open mindedness and a high degree of motivation and discipline. Before you turn down an idea, think again.

No one can provide you with a guaranteed Beat Inflation strategy. Therefore, use the ideas presented in this book to kick-start your own creative thinking. Even if an idea might not work for you, you may use it as a stepping stone to develop a new one that will.

THE FUNDAMENTALS: UNDERSTANDING THE CURRENT INFLATION PROBLEM

CHAPTER 1: FOUR DANGEROUS INFLATIONARY FORCES ARE AT WORK – A PERFECT INFLATION STORM IS POSSIBLE

There are four different forces contributing to higher inflation. It is important for you to familiarize yourself with these forces and to track their development. Should all four strengthen at the same time, we may be heading into a perfect inflation storm. While this may not happen, you need to be alert and prepared (like Florida residents when a hurricane is approaching). Being informed about future inflation scenarios will facilitate your work in your Beat Inflation team.

INFLATION FORCE 1: LOSS OF FAITH IN STABILITY

We tend to take the stability and reliability of paper money systems for granted. The overwhelming majority of people in developed countries expect not only that businesses will continue to accept their paper money, but also that we can (more or less) buy the same amount of goods with our money. Past inflation rates have been so low for such a long time that few people seriously worried about them. Until recently, high inflation was not a priority on corporate risk radar screens. Even record levels of debt, prolonged periods of fiscal overspending, and ultra-loose monetary policies have not dented our confidence in paper money systems.[5]

This is surprising if we look at the history of money in general and paper money systems in particular. Most paper money systems have not survived over time. A large number have failed and been replaced with new

---

[5] Paper money systems are also referred to as fiat money systems as they are not backed by real assets (e.g., gold).

paper money systems. Even the two major paper money systems that have survived for more than 200 years (the U.S. dollar and the British pound) do not show impressive stability. The purchasing power of both currencies today is only a fraction of what it was in the past (see Chart 4).

Chart 4: Loss of Purchasing Power of the U.S. Dollar

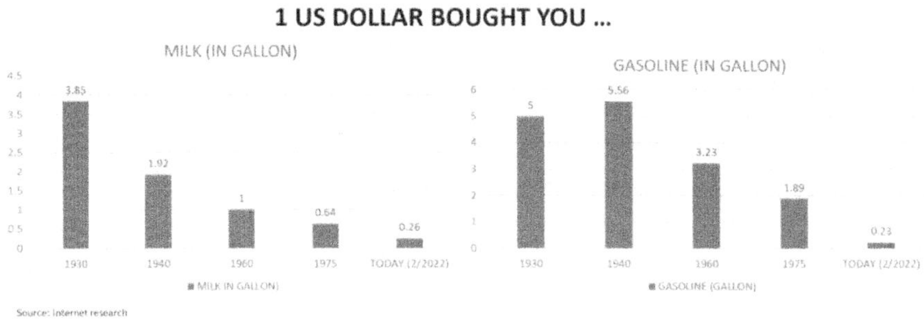

Paper money systems are based on confidence. As long as people have confidence in the system, it works well. As soon as this confidence starts to erode, inflation will accelerate. This is what I call Loss of Faith in Stability (LOFIS) inflation.

Chart 5 lists typical conditions that lead to a loss of faith in paper money systems.

Chart 5: Checklist of Requirements for LOFIS Inflation

Required input factor for LOFIS inflation	**Present today?**
Over-indebtedness of government (requiring low interest rates to avoid serious disruptions)	**Yes**
Prolonged periods of significant fiscal deficits	**Yes**
Expansionary monetary policies by central banks	**Yes**
Substantial amount of liquidity in the system	**Yes**
Perception of ineffective politicians and governments	**Yes**
Increasing negative perception of a country's future prospects (i.e., rising pessimism)	**Yes**
Weakening of exchange rate (leading to imported inflation)	**Depends on country**

As Chart 5 shows, we are facing perfect conditions for LOFIS inflation.

LOFIS inflation is dangerous as it does not respond well to tools used to fight ordinary inflation (e.g., aggressive hiking of interest rates). More has to be done to regain people's confidence in their country's central banks, politicians, and paper money system.

LOFIS inflation can spiral out of control as it did in Venezuela recently. At that point, interest rate hikes will become meaningless. People will give up on a currency and the central bank's promise to support it. Venezuelan businesses and consumers ditched their own currency and adopted one that is considered more stable: the U.S. dollar. This is a typical development when inflation spirals out of control. Needless to say, such developments add to the unfortunate trends of inequality and poverty.

We are at an early stage of LOFIS inflation. How bad it will become depends on the competence of a country's politicians and central bankers. The severity of the crisis will vary significantly by country.

Once LOFIS Inflation occurs, governments and central banks must act swiftly and decisively to regain credibility and stop the process. Unfortunately, upcoming elections and other factors may motivate decision makers to give in to populist demands of more spending and more debt. Such policy mistakes are unfortunately a common occurrence during LOFIS Inflation.

For example, U.S. decision makers failed to address the root causes that led to the inflation shocks of 1969 and 1973–1974. Unsurprisingly, inflation returned in 1977 in a more dramatic and vicious way and almost spiraled out of control.

It is important to stress that LOFIS inflation can occur despite significant economic weakness. Surprisingly, many economists were caught by surprise when the 1970s inflation cycle presented a simultaneous situation of low economic growth and high inflation. This phenomenon became known as "stagflation."

INFLATION FORCE 2: **E**MERGING **M**ARKETS **E**CONOMIC **G**ROWTH

The second inflationary force is quite different from LOFIS inflation. I call it **E**merging **M**arkets **E**conomic **G**rowth (EMEG) inflation. Chart 6 shows the difference between EMEG and LOFIS inflation.

Chart 6: EMEG and LOFIS Inflation

	EMEG Inflation (**E**merging **M**arkets **E**conomic **G**rowth)	**LOFIS Inflation** (**L**oss **of** **F**aith **i**n **S**tability)
Main Cause	Strong economic growth in populous emerging market countries	Loss of faith in paper money in developed countries
Drivers	• Increased demand for resources and products originating from strong growth in populous emerging market countries • Global demand exceeds global supply regardless of economic strength in (less populous) developed countries	• Loss of faith in long-term financial stability caused by excessive debt, fiscal deficits, ultra-loose monetary policies • Market participants fear that monetary reality does not match economic reality • People increasingly seek to preserve wealth by preferring real assets over monetary assets

Over the past three decades, we have witnessed a structural break in the world economy that will lead to tectonic shifts going forward. Emerging market countries are transforming themselves into economic powerhouses. To call this process an industrial revolution would be a gross understatement, as the speed of this transformation is about ten times as fast as the Industrial Revolution of the nineteenth and twentieth centuries in Europe. Even more important, the scale of this economic transformation is gigantic. While the Industrial Revolution encompassed several hundred million people at most, this period of economic leapfrogging is catapulting billions of people in emerging markets from poverty and simplicity into the lifestyles of modern middle-class consumers in developed countries.

Consequently, the demand for commodities, products, and services originating from emerging markets will increase dramatically over the years to come. Global supply will struggle to keep up with the additional demand, a development that most likely will lead to rising prices and inflation for both developed and emerging market countries. This is EMEG inflation.

We must not underestimate the impact of EMEG inflation on the world and the size and power of the factors driving it. Billions of people in emerging market countries are more or less on the road to becoming typical Western-style middle-class families that will build houses and buy cars, furniture, appliances, and other products of which their parents could have only dreamed. They will upgrade their nutrition preferences to consume a diet much richer in animal protein than that of their parents, leading to higher prices for meat and related products.

EMEG inflation is the result of changes in the demand-supply balance. Demand-driven inflation emerges when, due to strong economic growth in populous emerging markets countries, the demand for products and services outpaces available supply and capacities. In other words, relative scarcity of commodities, resources, products, and services leads to rising prices. This imbalance between demand and supply is structural in nature. Therefore, it may take more than a decade to restore an inflation-neutral equilibrium.

In the classic view of economics, this type of inflation was considered relatively harmless as governments and central banks possessed adequate tools to deal with the problem. Economic and monetary measures to cool down economic growth have proven effective to deal with traditional demand-driven inflation.

Today's situation is not only different, it is more complicated and dangerous for developed countries. EMEG inflation originates outside of their control spectrum (i.e., in emerging economies). Citizens in those emerging economies rightly claim their right to live like the middle class in developed countries.

Therefore, monetary measures (e.g., higher interest rates) in developed countries may prove ineffective and possibly harmful. Such policies may lead to a combination of lower economic growth and even higher inflation in developed countries. This, in turn, would weaken exchange rates. As a result, imports from emerging markets to the developed world would become even more expensive (i.e., imported inflation).

EMEG inflation is a dangerous threat. The scale and complexity of this problem is unprecedented. As more than four billion people contribute to EMEG inflation, developed countries need new approaches to deal with the consequences. Failure to react may mean a long-lasting period of elevated inflation.

INFLATION FORCE 3: GEOPOLITICAL CHANGES

Over the past decade we have noticed an accelerating new trend of deglobalization. The favored concept among politicians is "my country first." The clear and attractive benefits of globalization and global coordination are being ignored. Globalization is condemned as the main reason for many domestic economic problems.

De-globalization comes in many forms. It includes new tariffs, import and export restrictions, trade wars, and on-shoring. The latter seeks to bring back manufacturing activities from other countries despite cost disadvantages. Onshoring is pursued for two reasons. First, it is a way to ensure that critical products can be produced reliably domestically ("self-sufficiency"). Second, onshoring is often incentivized by governments to create domestic jobs and to improve a country's economy.

Unfortunately, decision makers fail to understand that de-globalization is a perfect boost for inflation. We are moving away from an efficient and effective system that has worked for a long time and created win-win situations in most cases. The classic business principle of finding optimum economies of scale will be abolished through de-globalization. This will lead to inefficient manufacturing structures around the world. Moving from a few, but large, manufacturing hubs to many, but smaller, ones will ultimately increase costs and product prices. It is not rocket science to understand that such trends will boost inflation and keep it high in the future.

Other geopolitical changes leading to more inflation are the recent tensions among key blocks of the global economy. The war in Ukraine has led to massive interruptions of supply chains and is contributing heavily to inflation. In addition, tensions in Asia (e.g., between China and Taiwan, between North Korea and South Korea) add to the concerns about supply chain disruptions and de-globalization.

Last, the understandable push to replace fossil fuel-based energy with sustainable energy sources will lead (at least initially) to higher prices in the mid-term. As these changes require massive investments in infrastructure projects, costs will be relatively high until innovation, scale, and accumulated experience enable an exploitation of new economies of scale.

INFLATION FORCE 4: 12 UNIQUE COMPLICATIONS

There are additional complications that we need to watch closely, which could derail economic, political, and social stability and lead to even more inflation in the future (see Chart 7).

These complications address many different issues that could significantly influence future inflation rates. I addressed most of these complications in chapter three of *The Return of High Inflation.*[6] As the predominant focus of this book is on managing inflation, I will list an updated list of complications and issues without explicit discussion.

I may, however, highlight complication number eleven: the financial derivatives market. This market is extremely big, complex, and fragile. Its notional value is a multiple of world GDP. This market has never been tested by a period of high inflation. Consequently, we are exposed to a potentially severe risk with unknown dimension. I have highlighted this danger in past publications and presentations. I personally consider it the Achilles heel of the modern financial system.

---

[6] See Hammes (2016), The Return of High Inflation, chapter three.

Chart 7: 12 Complications Contributing to Higher Inflation, Risks, and Disruptions

No.	Complication contributing to higher inflation and higher risks
1	Global synchronization of loose monetary policies and fiscal overspending offer no place to hide.
2	Last inflation crisis ended forty years ago – there is little if no practical inflation management experience among decision makers in public office, business, and the financial industry.
3	Global indebtedness problem is not war-related (as in the past), it is structural. Hence, it will be hard to reverse.
4	Most of debt issued used for consumption and financial engineering, not for investments into innovation and productivity.
5	Explosive growth of complexity in economic, financial, and social systems creates severe risk management challenges during the next crisis.
6	Financial markets operate at lightning speed and will be difficult to contain and stabilize during an inflation crisis.
7	Current business and financial infrastructure systems are not built to withstand inflation.
8	Most decision makers in politics, business, and finance have not experienced inflation in the past. Policy mistakes are likely.
9	Central banks' procedures may prove ineffective as a large part of inflation originates from other countries or is structural in nature.
10	Our "everything just-in-time economy" makes supply chains and inventories vulnerable to inflation disruptions.
11	Our financial derivatives markets have never been tested by a period of high inflation. Particularly, the interest rate derivatives market may contribute to increased volatility.
12	A new era of nationalism, suspension of international trade agreements, and de-globalization creates strong inflationary forces.

CHAPTER 2: INFLATION MANAGEMENT – UNDERSTANDING THE BIG PICTURE

The previous chapter introduced you to four powerful inflationary forces. The key questions are: Will they coincide? Will there be counteracting forces taming future inflation? Will politicians and central bankers implement prudent strategies to tackle inflation?

In this chapter, we are going to put the four inflationary forces into perspective. A look back to the 1970s inflation crisis will help us do so. The goal is to understand how inflation works and how it affects businesses and individuals.

As mentioned before, a perfect inflation storm could occur if the four inflationary forces coincide and create positive feedback loops. It would be difficult for decision makers in politics, central banks, and businesses to control such a development. This is our worst-case scenario. You can call it a long-lasting inflation tsunami.

However, other, more benign, scenarios are possible as well, particularly if regulators and politicians react with prudence and competence and avoid past mistakes. Global coordination would help as well. Unfortunately, this seems an unlikely outcome for the current situation.

We should expect different inflation outcomes for different countries, as vulnerability varies considerably. Therefore, readers should watch their country's specific situation closely and implement appropriate countermeasures should inflation rates become excessive. In the following chapters we will discuss many ideas that could be part of your personal Beat Inflation strategy.

We also need to understand that inflation is not a static problem, but a dynamic one. This is an important point that is often neglected, even by top executives of large companies. Therefore, strategic agility is a key requirement to do well during a period of high inflation.

In a simplified world, an inflation period goes through four generic phases that are described in my FPIM model. I developed this model for my consulting work with corporate clients. However, it can be used by the general public as well to help track inflation as it moves from phase to phase. The model facilitates strategy formulation and helps us navigate through these volatile times.

The most important point is that each inflation phase is different than the previous one. Therefore, each phase requires a new strategy that targets the issues specific to each phase. Failing to anticipate a new phase of an inflation period can have disastrous consequences.

The FPIM model is shown in Chart 8. A detailed description of the complete model appears in the Appendix.[7]

---

[7] The text in the Appendix is a reprint from my 2016 book *The Return of High Inflation*.

CHART 8: THE FOUR PHASES INFLATION MANAGEMENT MODEL

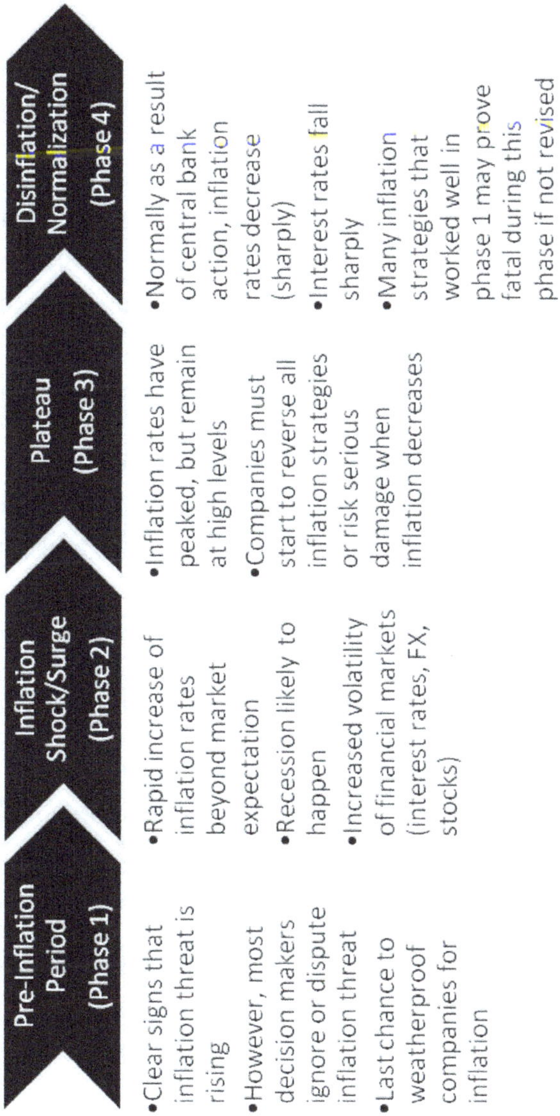

Chart 8 shows a generic inflation cycle that moves from one phase to the next without interruptions or complications. In actuality, variations do occur, generally as the result of:

- Competence of decision makers in politics and central banks and the quality of their decision making
- Coordination between politicians and central bankers
- Behavior of the general public (e.g., strikes, election results)
- Circumstantial factors

Competent decision makers can greatly reduce the pain inflation inflicts on the economy and the general public. However, this long-term gain will come with short-term pain. Politicians are often not willing to accept such a trade-off. Instead, they choose popular measures to gain greater support for the next election. Such policy mistakes by politicians and central banks can lead to a much longer and more painful inflation period.

Let us return to the FPIM model. Chart 9 illustrates the dramatic changes that occur when the economy moves from one inflation phase to the next. These changes require significant and prudent adoptions of our Beat Inflation strategy. What might have been a good strategy in phase one may lead to catastrophic consequences in phase two.

In general, phase two, inflation shock, is the most dangerous, as the economy goes from boom to recession.

The inflation shock of 1973-1974 was particularly severe. Decision makers in politics, central banks, and businesses were caught unprepared by the sudden rise of inflation. The S&P 500 stock market index lost about half of its value during this period.

CHART 9: Economic Conditions May Change Dramatically During an Inflation Period

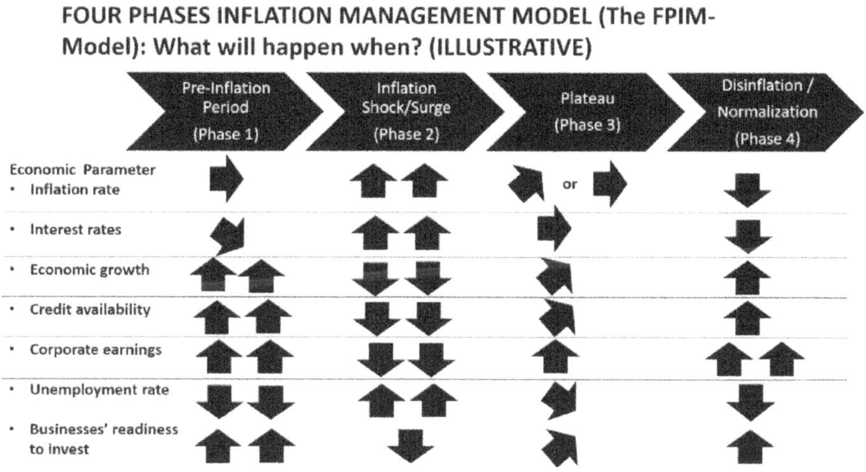

INFLATION ROLLERCOASTER RIDES

Unfortunately, a country can get caught in a long-lasting inflation period if central bankers and politicians fail to implement the appropriate responses to address inflation. In such cases, phases two and three may drag on over extended periods of time. Alternatively, it is also possible that an economy that already reached phase four ("disinflation/normalization") may experience an inflation relapse that brings it back to phase two ("inflation shock"). This happened to the U.S. economy when inflation rates rose from 4.9 % in 1976 to 13.3 % in 1979. This was the second severe inflation shock of the 1970s.[8]

[8] Note: There was an additional inflation shock in 1969. In total, the U.S. experienced three inflation shocks during the so-called 1970s inflation crisis.

In a worst-case scenario, decision makers fail to contain inflation and price increases spiral out of control. This happened during the German period of hyperinflation (1923-1924) and, more recently, in Venezuela.

The 1970s inflation period was a great example of central bankers and politicians failing to time their action steps. When inflation was rising they acted too late and too aggressively. When their excessive action created a severe recession, they acted too early and too forcefully to kick-start an economic recovery.

In other words, the 1970s inflation crisis was a game of ambulance chasing that created substantial and unnecessary economic and financial volatility. Great pain had to be endured by businesses and the general public.

Chart 10 shows rollercoasting inflation rates due to poor decision making by politicians and central bankers. Note that each inflation peak tops the previous one.

Chart 10: Three Waves of Inflation in the U.S. During the 1960s and 1970s[9]

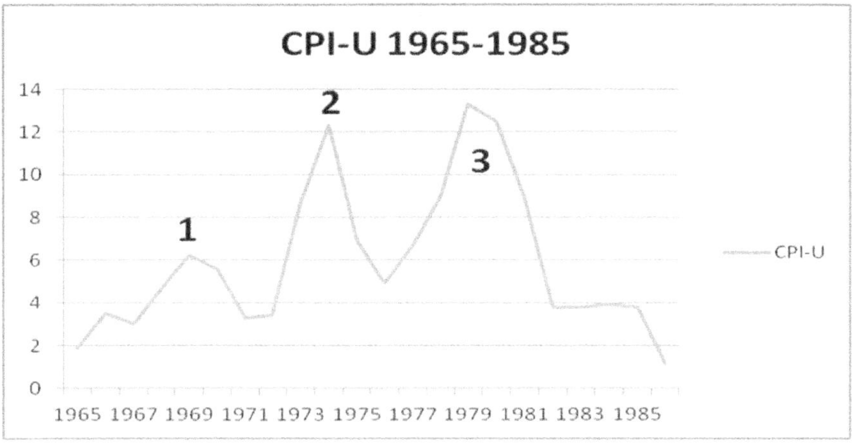

Not surprisingly, rollercoasting inflation rates led to a rollercoasting U.S. economy as Chart 11 illustrates. The grey shaded areas indicate periods of recessions.

[9] Hammes, *The Return of High Inflation* (2016), p. 36.

Chart 11: A Rollercoasting U.S. Economy During the 1970s Inflation Crisis

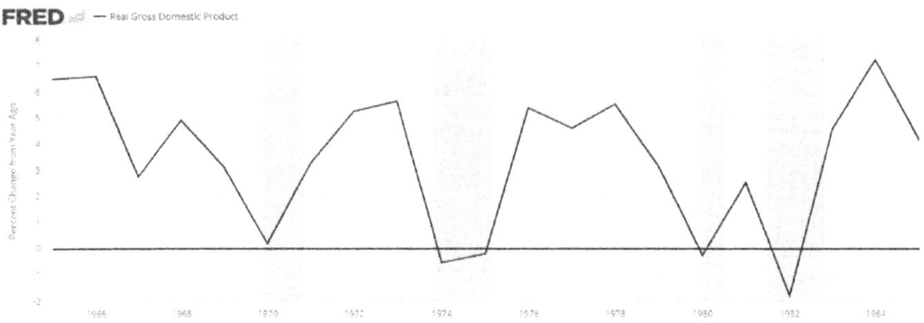

Source: U.S. Bureau of Economic Analysis, Real Gross Domestic Product [GDPC1], retrieved from FRED, Federal Reserve Bank of St. Louis; https://fred.stlouisfed.org/series/GDPC1, July 31, 2022.

Chart 11 has two messages for us. First, rollercoasting economic growth created a severe strategic challenge for businesses and the general public. Strategies had to be revised constantly to reflect new economic realities. It took sometimes less than two years for the U.S. economy to go from a high growth period to a full-blown recession.

Second, the chart shows that using the term "stagflation" to describe the 1970s inflation crisis is misleading. The U.S. economy had never been stagnant during the 1970s; rather, it was extremely volatile. Therefore, stagflation should be replaced by the term "recesflation," an economy with frequent recessionary periods accompanied by high inflation rates.

Let us look more closely at the recessionary periods of the 1970s. It is fair to classify these recessions as quite severe (see Chart 12). We should keep this in mind when preparing for today's inflation challenges. Even in 2022, too many people are too optimistic, hoping for a "soft landing" of the economy without experiencing a severe recession. Judging from the 1970s experience, such expectations seem unrealistic.

Chart 12: Recessionary Periods During the 1970s Inflation Crisis[10]

Start (first quarter in recession)	End (last quarter in recession)	Duration
Q2 1969	Q4 1970	6 quarter
Q4 1973	Q1 1975	5 quarter
Q2 1979	Q2 1980	5 quarter
Q2 1981	Q2 1982	5 quarter

It is important to add that interest rates also followed a rollercoaster pattern. The Federal Reserve resorted to quite dramatic interest rate responses during the 1970s inflation crisis. In my view, this hyper-activity greatly contributed to "rollercoaster inflation" and "rollercoaster economic growth" outcomes. Chart 13 shows the development of the federal funds rate during this period.

---

[10] Hamilton, James, Dates of U.S. recessions as inferred by GDP-based recession indicator [JHDUSRGDPBR], retrieved from FRED, Federal Reserve Bank of St. Louis; https://fred.stlouisfed.org/series/JHDUSRGDPBR, March 30, 2022.

Chart 13: Federal Funds Rate Between 1965 and 1984[11]

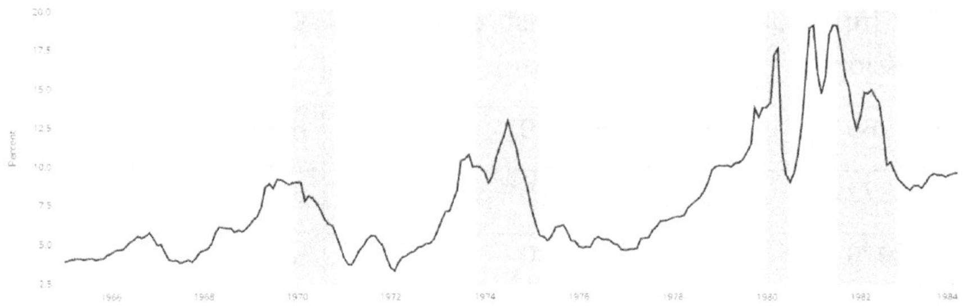

Rollercoaster interest rates were a great challenge for both businesses and individuals, with interest rates for lending products (e.g., mortgages) fluctuating dramatically. Picking the right time for any financing decision was like playing the lottery.

There is a significant difference between the situation then and now: the level of indebtedness. Global indebtedness is roughly three times as high as it was during the early 1970s.[12] High debt levels limit central banks' maneuverability. If banks raise interest rates too much, they could trigger a severe recession and banking crisis.

However, even less extreme interest rate hikes run the risk of causing severe credit defaults and recessions. High debt levels work like an amplifier for any interest rate move.

The volatile economic period of the 1970s provides us with valuable lessons learned. We must familiarize ourselves with this particular inflation crisis as it provides valuable insights into inflation mechanics and dynamics. For those readers seeking a deeper understanding of this period, please see Chapter 10 in my 2016 book *The Return of High Inflation*.

---

[11] Source: St. Louis Federal Reserve website

[12] Based on IMF data on global indebtedness and own estimates

THE END OF HIGH INFLATION PERIODS

There are different views on how to best fight inflation. Most experts believe that the implementation of restrictive monetary policies (i.e., higher interest rates and less liquidity provided to markets) is sufficient. This hypothesis, however, is not supported by the events of the 1970s inflation crisis. Twice, inflation returned to the U.S. economy after a period of restrictive monetary policies.

When inflation was defeated in 1982, something else had happened. In addition to the Federal Reserve's tightening, politicians became more actively involved. In addition, new developments in international business provided strong deflationary tailwinds. The following developments played a decisive role to bring down inflation and to keep it low for about forty years (i.e., until 2021):

- President Reagan's political program (often referred to as "Reaganomics") led to deregulation (lower costs to companies), greater flexibility, higher productivity, and lower taxes.
- Computerization (both hardware and software innovations) spread across the country leading to higher productivity and significant cost reductions.
- Globalization reduced manufacturing costs substantially.
- Outsourcing strategies helped reduce administrative and manufacturing costs. Global supply chains made manufacturing more cost-efficient.
- University-educated managers (e.g., M.B.A.s) helped push through management reforms that improved companies' productivity and efficiency. Management became more systematic and professional.

It is quite likely that in the absence of these developments, inflation rates would have bounced back again during the early 1980s.

Therefore, decision makers in politics, central banks, and businesses are well advised to focus not only on monetary policies when fighting high inflation, but, in particular, on the following goals:

- Improve productivity
- Restart globalization
- Implement business-friendly policies
- Encourage innovativeness that leads to higher productivity, more efficiency, and higher effectiveness
- Strengthen the education system to provide talent needed to make businesses and processes more efficient, effective, and innovative.

In my view, today's high inflation will not be contained unless politicians and central bankers implement these changes. Therefore, monitoring policies implemented by central bankers and politicians and comparing these policies to these requirements will help us anticipate future inflation scenarios. If you do not see politicians and central bankers follow the path outlined in this chapter, you should be cautious in expecting an early end of the inflation crisis.

CONCLUSION:

Let me summarize the most important topics discussed in the first two chapters before we move on to the development of your personal Beat Inflation program:

- There are four different inflationary forces at work; each one is strong enough to keep inflation rates at excessive levels
- A perfect inflation storm is possible if several or all inflationary forces coincide (worst-case scenario)
- Inflation is a dynamic problem. The FPIM model is a tool that may help us navigate through these volatile and uncertain times
- There is a great risk of policy mistakes committed by politicians and central bankers. Such mistakes can increase the severity and duration of the inflation crisis.

CHAPTER 3: HOW AND WHERE INFLATION IMPACTS YOU

Most people make a dangerous mistake when preparing for a period of high inflation: They predominantly focus on their investment activities. Even worse, they wrongly believe that there is a magic investment that not only provides effective, comprehensive, and long-term protection against inflation risks (an "inflation flu shot"), but also makes them rich. Unfortunately, this magic investment does not exist.

Focusing only on your investment decisions will leave many more important issues and threats unaddressed. My experience suggests that for most people, their job provides the primary financial resources to pay monthly expenses and to save for retirement. Therefore, losing your job during a period of high inflation is one of the biggest short-term inflation risks (unless your investment income substantially outsizes your income from employment).

Therefore, the question "What is the best investment during periods of high inflation?" is not only the wrong question, it is also a misleading one. The more appropriate question is: What activities are required to prevent inflation having a negative impact on myself and my family? This quickly leads to a series of additional questions: How can I secure my current job? How can I obtain salary increases that offset actual inflation? How can I cut my spending? Should I prepare for national or international relocation if inflation and economic circumstances spin out of control?

These important questions need to be addressed in the context of your Beat Inflation strategy. Your inflation response must address a multitude of issues touching many different aspects of your life.

To address the many different aspects and requirements for best-practice inflation management, I have created a framework that encompasses five essential elements of a Beat Inflation strategy (see Chart 14). As you can see, wealth management issues are only one of the five elements.

CHART 14: The Five Elements of a Beat Inflation Strategy

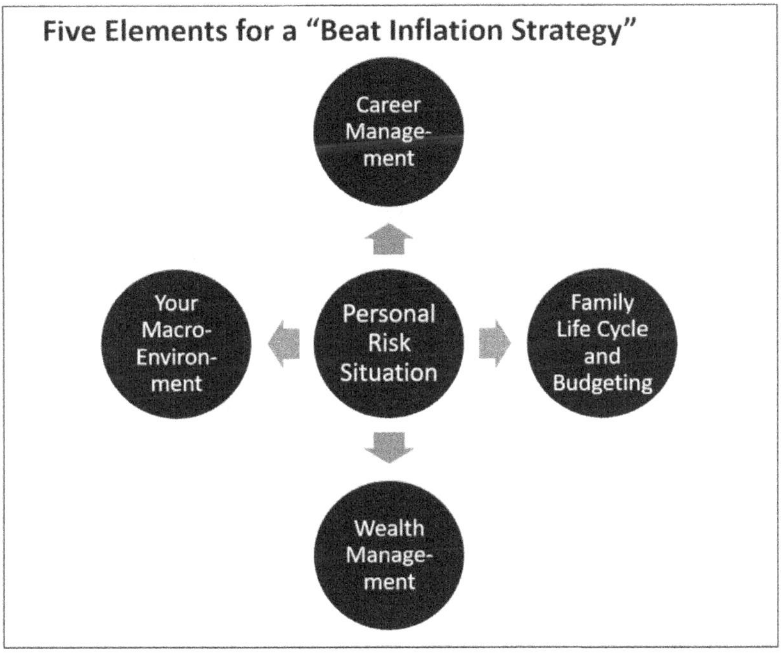

You must address the key issues for each element by answering the following questions:

- What are the key issues and risks you are exposed to?
- What is your worst-case scenario?
- What opportunities could you exploit?
- What are the action steps you need to implement to address all relevant issues and risks?

Let us discuss each element in more detail.

ELEMENT 1: PERSONAL RISK SITUATION

Risk is the possibility that an adverse event will lead to personal losses, damages, injuries, or other negative outcomes. The important word is "possibility." While a specific risk event may happen, it does not need to happen. Risk management is the activity that protects us from such adverse developments and their consequences.

The starting point for developing your personal Beat Inflation strategy is a detailed analysis of your personal risk situation. This is a very individualized task. Your risk situation is different from that of your friend's and requires tailor-made strategies to be successful. Do not copy other people's risk management strategies unless you have analyzed them in detail and conclude that it is appropriate to do so.

Most people neglect risk management activities until an actual risk event has occurred. However, once the damage has been done you cannot reverse it. The key success factor in risk management is to prepare diligently before a risk event materializes. Only early preparedness and anticipation will protect you and may give you a competitive edge.

For example, past high inflation periods typically led to significantly higher unemployment rates. We experienced this pattern during the 1970s inflation crisis in the U.S. The good news is that unemployment spikes occur with a time lag to spikes of inflation rates, allowing you time to prepare for a worsening job market. Your preparedness is based on two major activities: First, securing your current job by making you hard to replace, and second, pursuing strategies that increase your personal bargaining power to achieve salary increases that, at a minimum, match actual inflation rates. We will discuss these strategies in Chapter 8.

Understanding and actively managing your personal risk situation should be an ongoing high priority activity and not confined to periods of high inflation.

Unfortunately, many people are uncomfortable thinking about the risks in their lives. I assume that the widespread approach of positive thinking may be responsible for this unfortunate development. It is uncomfortable to think about things that could go wrong and may lead to financial setbacks. It is much more appealing to entertain positive thoughts about future prospects. While this is understandable, it exposes a person to significant unaddressed risks.

Therefore, it is important to remember that while positive thinking may make you feel good (in the short term), it puts you in a dangerous situation of high unpreparedness for adverse developments. We know too well from risk management history that the worst disasters happen when unpreparedness meets a severe risk event. Such a situation is typically a recipe for disaster, especially during periods of high inflation.

LIFE LESSON:

When risk events meet up with unpreparedness in life, it is typically a recipe for disaster. This is particularly true for periods of high inflation. Good preparedness can deal even with major risk events.

To avoid this dangerous situation, you should prepare for the worst and hope for the best.

To develop your personal risk strategy, you may find the following three categories helpful:

1. Your risk appetite (how much risk do I feel comfortable with?)
2. Your risk management capabilities (how good am I at managing a particular risk?)
3. Your risk absorption capacity (given my resources, how much risk can I absorb without facing unacceptable hardship or existential consequences?)

Assessing these three areas will improve the process of making consequential life decisions in general, and during periods of high inflation in particular. The framework should help you limit your risk taking to levels that you are comfortable with and equipped for. Chart 15 describes the three categories in more detail.

Chart 15: Understanding Your Personal Risk Situation

Category	Examples
Risk Appetite	• How much risk do I want to expose myself or my family to? • What are the key risks that I consider catastrophic or severe and which I should avoid at any price (e.g., loss of job, X percent loss of savings)? • At what risk level would I have problems sleeping well at night? • Am I emotionally prepared to accept the potential negative consequences if a high-risk strategy I chose fails?
Risk Management Skills	• Do I have the qualifications and experience to deal with the risks I am exposed to? Do I need external advice to do so? • What is my past risk management track record? Do I correctly assess my risk management skills or do I tend to over- (under-) rate them? • Collect past examples of well-managed risks and risk management failures. What is the balance between the two? Do I have a positive track record?
Risk Absorption Capacity	• Do I have fallback options available if my risk strategy fails (e.g., additional sources of income, savings)? • For how many dependents am I financially responsible? What does this mean for my risk absorption capacity? • For what future expenses will I need cash reserves (e.g., education, health care, significant house repairs)? • How many months would my savings support me and my dependents in case of job loss and rising price levels? Am I comfortable with this situation?

It is important to understand that life is inherently risky. We cannot and should not eliminate all risks in our lives. In fact, total risk elimination would lead to new and potentially bigger risks. Imagine never leaving your house anymore for fear of something bad that could happen.

Also, the higher our ambition level the more risks we need to take. With few exceptions, this rule applies to all aspects of life. However, you should not expose yourself to risks that you feel uncomfortable with. This should be the key rule guiding you through risky periods in life.

ELEMENT 2: CAREER MANAGEMENT

The main goal of career management during periods of high inflation is to obtain a secure income that increases (at a minimum) with actual inflation rates. Most likely, your job provides the main financial resources to pay living expenses. Therefore, securing your job and having the bargaining power to demand salary increases that offset inflation are the most important parts of your Beat Inflation strategy.

Chart 16: The Goals of Professional Career Management

Professional career management has two important goals during periods of high inflation: 1. Secure your job 2. Achieve salary increases that, at a minimum, offset inflation

Both tasks are demanding, given that periods of high inflation typically coincide with low economic growth (or recessions) and higher unemployment. During the 1970s inflation crisis, the U.S. experienced several recessions and spikes of unemployment rates. During the worst periods, unemployment rates crossed the 10% mark.

Just keeping your job may not be enough to maintain your current living standards. If you do not increase your salary to offset inflation, you are exposed to a growing inflation gap; that is, the difference between the growth rate of your expenses versus the growth rate of your income.

The inflation gap can grow to dangerous levels once inflation spirals out of control. A look back in inflation history explains why.

The period of German hyperinflation (1921-1923) had a disastrous impact on most middle- and lower-class families. Many endured severe poverty, including those highly educated individuals with respected careers (e.g., university professors, museum directors, senior public servants). They experienced these miserable conditions even though many were still employed.

The issue was that their employers did not raise their salaries in line with inflation rates. These individuals were not considered mission critical for the economy or their employers. If they left their jobs, they could have been easily replaced. In other words, these people did not have enough bargaining power to enforce inflation-offsetting salary increases.

High inflation treats people brutally. Past achievements and status do not guarantee future prosperity and success. The more intense inflation becomes, the greater the importance of bargaining power vis-à-vis your employer. Otherwise, your income will not enable you and your family to maintain your lifestyle and standard of living.

Bargaining power comes from a variety of sources and, in general, is the result of the following factors:

- The importance of your job and your personal contribution to the overall success of a company or organization
- The difficulty of finding a replacement for you
- The specificity and depth of your skill portfolio
- Your network of meaningful relationships to clients, vendors, or regulators
- Your social role in the organization

A successful Beat Inflation strategy must focus on raising your bargaining power with your current employer and, possibly, identifying alternative employers (just in case). A mission-critical employee who is also highly sought by competitors has little to fear during periods of high inflation.

For example, while a highly trained plumber is mission critical for a plumbing company, an office assistant in the same company is unlikely to be so. The first brings in revenue, the second does not. However, the person managing and maintaining a crucial computer system in a company is mission critical, even if they do not generate any direct revenue.

Correctly assessing your bargaining power is a key activity everyone should conduct regularly. Keep in mind that your bargaining power is not a constant. It can be improved through targeted action. For example, taking classes that teach you relevant and marketable skills (e.g., computer programming) can quickly improve your bargaining power at a substantial rate.

Many people will remain employed, but fail to secure sufficient salary increases to offset rising inflation. In such situations, it is helpful to supplement your income and avoid drawing down your savings to fill the inflation gap. Luckily, there are many different ways available to accomplish this. We will discuss concrete ideas as part of the DVBI program later.

ELEMENT 3: FAMILY LIFE CYCLE AND BUDGETING

History suggests that inflation periods can last an extended period of time. For example, the 1970s inflation crisis lasted for about a decade before it was put under control. Therefore, it is important to base your Beat Inflation strategy not only on the current situation, but also on anticipated changes in your family life cycle and related spending needs.

Future family events may have a significant impact on your financial budgeting and long-term financial planning. Such events include:

- Your children may attend an expensive college/university and are unlikely to receive financial assistance.
- You are transitioning to retirement.
- You plan to get married and start a family.
- Your growing family requires a move to a bigger (and more expensive) house.
- Your age and/or medical status suggests a greater need for expensive medical treatment over the next decade.

It is important that you anticipate future family events and their impact on your financial condition as clearly and in as much detail as possible. Doing so enables you to implement corrective action before a financial need requires you to do so.

Financial budgeting becomes extremely important during periods of high inflation. Because such periods are commonly preceded by periods of economic booms and investment success, people easily fall into the trap of assuming an eternal financial bliss and ignore the need for rigorous financial planning and budgeting. The reality is that the earlier you practice active cost management the lesser the pain later. For most people, high inflation will be a negative event that requires spending cuts, strict cost control, and more prudent financial planning.

ELEMENT 4: YOUR MACROENVIRONMENT

One important element of a successful Beat Inflation strategy is often neglected: the analysis of your current macroenvironment. If you live in a region or country that is particularly hard hit by high inflation, a strategic analysis of mobility options needs to be part of your personal inflation strategy.

Sometimes, moving to a different region within a country can create a significant improvement. However, a whole country may be drawn down by an inflation crisis. For example, many Venezuelans were caught unprepared when inflation spiraled out of control about a decade ago. Although many received excellent education, pursued professional careers, and practiced conservative financial planning, Venezuela at that time offered very limited opportunities for such individuals. In addition, political and social stability eroded, leading to unacceptable crime rates, a deteriorating infrastructure, poor medical support, and scarcity of crucial products. Many people emigrated to different countries seeking better living conditions. However, this option was available only for those ready and prepared to make an international move.

Mobility can be an effective strategic response to excessively high inflation and its life-changing consequences; however, relocation requires diligent and careful preparation. It can take years to fulfill all requirements for an international move, including obtaining valid visas, meeting new job requirements (e.g., certifications), learning a new language, and building a new professional and social network.

When analyzing the attractiveness of your geographical location, you should not assume that high inflation is a transitory problem. Because an inflation crisis may turn into a social and political crisis as well, excessive optimism about inflation problems disappearing soon may backfire dramatically. Emigration and mobility windows may shut down, requiring you to sit out a crisis that may last a generation. For example, Germany's path from one disaster to another after experiencing hyperinflation in the early 1920s lasted more than three decades before reverting back to normal.

While regional or international relocation is a cumbersome activity, it may also be a worthwhile strategy in the long term. New friendships are established, new skills are learned (e.g., languages), and new life philosophies are adopted. Therefore, despite initial hardship, international mobility often leads to substantial personal growth and much improved situations for all family members.

ELEMENT 5: WEALTH MANAGEMENT

Protecting your savings and wealth during periods of high inflation is an equally important and difficult challenge. Inflation cycles occur along with headwinds in the economy and high volatility in financial markets. Under such conditions, it is not easy to achieve an investment return that fully offsets actual inflation. The challenge is even bigger if you calculate your investment return on a post-tax basis.

During the 1970s inflation crisis, accumulated inflation was about 130%. In other words, over a period of about ten years, you needed to achieve an investment return of 130% on your assets to break even. In fact, you needed to achieve a much higher return if you included taxes in your assessment (e.g., on capital gains, dividends, and interest income).

To put this into perspective, the S&P 500 returned about 89% during that time period (pre-tax calculation including dividends). Obviously, the stock market did not fully protect you from inflation at that time.

Wealth management during periods of high inflation is particularly difficult for the following reasons:

1. **Widespread irrationality:** An inflation surge often catches the majority of decision makers in politics, business, regulatory organizations, the financial world, and the general public by surprise and in a state of unpreparedness. This can lead to a situation of significant emotional confusion and anger.
   We know from history that collective unpreparedness for a risk event coupled with high levels of confusion and anger can lead to irrational decision making, emotional overreactions, and erratic developments.

2. **Lack of inflation management competence:** The last severe inflation crisis in the developed world began in 1973 and ended in 1982. It is fair to assume that most decision makers and a large part of the general public have very limited practical experience with inflation management issues.

3. **Complexity of today's world:** Modern Western development occurred with an over-proportional increase in complexity. Systems that build the infrastructure and foundation of our daily conduct have become extremely interconnected, complicated, fragile, and hard to manage.
   Therefore, external shocks (as well as internal malfunctions) pose a severe threat to the normal functioning of these systems. The key issue is that we can neither accurately predict the consequences to an external shock nor can we confidently assume that decision makers can control the functioning of these systems. An external shock

such as high inflation may lead to a situation in which the systems control us rather than we control the systems.

4. **High inflation and structural breaks:** In statistics, a structural break describes an event that abruptly changes past patterns, trends, and relationships among aggregates and elements of a system. This can lead to significant forecasting and planning errors and flawed decision making. Given our historic experiences, inflation is likely to create one or several severe structural breaks in the world of investments. Structural breaks are both difficult to predict and difficult to deal with. Before new and clear patterns and trends emerge, we may experience a period of erraticism and dangerous volatility. These unpredictable periods precede the establishment of a "new normal" of causation, trends, and inter-relationships in the world of investments.

5. **Unpredictability of political, regulatory, business, and financial decision making:** The future is the result of prior periods' decision making. The way politicians, CEOs, regulators, and investors think about inflation determines their decision making, which, in turn, greatly shapes future outcomes. Although no one can read minds and predict the quality of decision making, we know from history that severe policy mistakes are a common occurrence during periods of high inflation and that such decisions have an enormous impact on the performance and predictability of many investment categories.

These issues remind us that investment decisions during periods of high inflation are exposed to high uncertainty and are dependent on the specific situational context at a given time. Strategies that work in country A may not work at all in country B. Therefore, it is important to discuss investment strategies with a qualified professional and to create a tailor-made solution that reflects your risk-taking preferences and limitations.

A book can describe only in general terms how inflation has impacted different investment categories. It cannot provide the dynamic type of help needed to respond to new developments. This is the reason why investment strategies are not part of the DVBI program. This task should be undertaken with a qualified professional in a dynamic process reacting to new developments as they occur.

Although no one can predict the performance of financial markets during periods of high inflation with great certainty, there are some patterns in how different asset classes have performed in the past. It may be worthwhile to be aware of these generic patterns that are mostly derived from past inflation periods.

Chart 17 describes the attractiveness of different investments during each respective phase of an inflation cycle. It uses the author's FPIM model to depict performance patterns observed in previous inflation periods. The idea is that inflation is not a static occurrence, but moves through four different phases:

- Phase 1: Pre-inflation period
- Phase 2: Inflation shock/surge
- Phase 3: Plateau
- Phase 4: Disinflation/normalization

Although I developed the model for my strategy consulting work with corporate clients, it also helps us to think through the changing conditions for different investment classes and to move from a static to a more dynamic investment strategy. The latter is likely to be more suitable to deal with the enormous level of erraticism and volatility during periods of high inflation.

Chart 17: Investment Conditions Depending on the Stage of an Inflation Cycle (Illustrative)

	Phase of inflation cycle			
Asset Class	**Phase 1 Pre-Inflation Period**	**Phase 2 Inflation Shock/Surge**	**Phase 3 Plateau**	**Phase 4 Disinflation/ Normalization**
Stocks	++	- -	+	++
Bonds	+	- -	+	++
Gold	+/-	++	+	- -
Commodities	+/-	+	++	- -
Real Estate	+/-	+/-	+	+
Long-term fixed savings accounts	+/-	- -	- -	++
Cash	-	+/-	-	-
FX investments in safe harbor countries	+/-	++	++	--

Legend (range): ++: highly attractive; -- highly unattractive (illustrative and simplified assessment)

Past experience suggests that every investment asset performs differently during each phase of an inflation cycle. For example, stocks may underperform during Phase 2 (inflation shock) should companies and investors get caught unprepared by inflation (leading to higher interest rates and lower economic growth). However, stocks may out-perform once inflation has been brought under control. While bonds typically underperform during periods of rising interest rates (i.e., phase 2), long-term fixed rate bonds may out-perform after inflation has reached its peak and interest rates are falling (i.e., phase 4).

In summary, each investment seems to have its time to shine during an inflation cycle and its time to underperform. Therefore, a dynamic approach using this model may help investors make more thoughtful decisions.[13]

[13] A detailed discussion of the performance and issues of different asset classes during periods of high inflation can be found in Chapter 14 of my book *The Return of High Inflation*.

FIGHT BACK AT INFLATION: THE DOUBLE VICTORY BEAT INFLATION PROGRAM (DVBI-PROGRAM)

CHAPTER 4: CHOOSE A TEAM APPROACH WHEN ATTACKING INFLATION

Inflation affects our lives in multiple ways. We need to consider inflation issues when making professional career decisions, budgeting our household expenses, or making financing and investment decisions. It is almost like fighting a war on multiple fronts. This can be confusing, frustrating, and overwhelming. Most of us do not have inflation management experience. It is a new risk we are exposed to and we have received very limited training in dealing with it.

When people are exposed to new severe risks or caught in a crisis situation, it is rarely a good idea to address the situation completely on your own. If you choose isolation, you may quickly end up being overwhelmed, afraid, and, as a consequence, paralyzed. You may become fatalistic and lose the energy and motivation needed to address these problems and turn some of the risks into a great opportunity.

Scientists suggest that we do better when addressing complex problems as a team. Therefore, I highly recommend adopting a team approach when tackling inflation challenges. Specifically, I recommend forming Beat Inflation teams. Get together with a select group of friends, colleagues, or relatives and fight these challenges together. Doing so will increase your motivation, provide mutual support during tough times, and strengthen your confidence. The team approach is likely to develop better solutions and strategies, particularly if the team consists of members with diverse skill profiles and backgrounds. You can use the team to brainstorm an inflation problem or to critique each other's strategies.

Do not face inflation management challenges alone. Get together with others and create your own Beat Inflation team. Meet weekly to discuss your progress implementing the DVBI program.

Take a minute to think about the people you will ask to join your Beat Inflation team and write down their names:

1)

2)

3)

4)

5)

6)

7)

8)

9)

10)

11)

To increase motivation, mood, and energy, consider the task of beating inflation as a social reality game. The goal for you and your team is to slay the inflation dragon; that is, to fully eliminate your personal inflation gap. Trust me, this activity can actually be a rewarding, educational, and fun-creating experience. You also may make new friends or strengthen existing relationships. If we turn the otherwise demotivating task of beating inflation into a game, we may get an additional motivational boost. You can create a poster that tracks the team's progress and update it in your team meeting. And of course, you should celebrate milestone achievements with your team.

THE GOAL: BEAT INFLATION AND HAVE FUN DOING SO

The first step is to build your Beat Inflation team. Your team can include family members, friends, or colleagues that will fight jointly against the inflation dragon. It should consist of people with diverse backgrounds in terms of skills and professional experience. You may wish to start with a smaller number of people and then gradually expand. At no time should you be on your own. Your group will support you and you will support your group. One for all and all for one.

Adding a social dimension to this project has several advantages. You will feel more motivated to work diligently on the inflation issues you are facing. As a team, you can learn from each other, discuss new ideas, or help each other during times of setbacks. You can also leverage each other's experiences, backgrounds, and skills when discussing and implementing new ideas. You can delegate research tasks to members of the team. And, you will have more fun along the way.

Therefore, you should set up a group of five or more people and agree on the following action steps:

- Meeting frequency (ideally, weekly)
- Meeting mode (in person, video conference)
- Communication (e.g., create a group chat on your phone or social media)
- Meeting logistics (find a quiet place for in-person meetings or obtain appropriate software for video calls)

Your Beat Inflation team is the forum to ask questions and to share new ideas. During your meetings you will discuss progress to date, next steps, and new issues you are facing. In each meeting, you will discuss progress based on the four core activities of the DVBI program. If you add additional activities, you will discuss these as well.

It is important to be organized. Therefore, one person should take notes of planned action steps, deliverables, responsibilities, and progress to date. You may rotate the responsibility for creating these meeting protocols.

THREE PERFORMANCE LEVELS FOR THE BEAT INFLATION GAME

The goal of the game is simple: eliminate the inflation gap. You want to avoid expenses that increase faster than your income. In other words, you want (at a minimum) to retain your current standard of living. Ideally, you will over-compensate for the additional costs of inflation and turn inflation into an opportunity that increases your standard of living.

In general, participants can achieve three different mastery levels (see Chart 18).

CHART 18: Three Performance Levels for Your DVBI Game

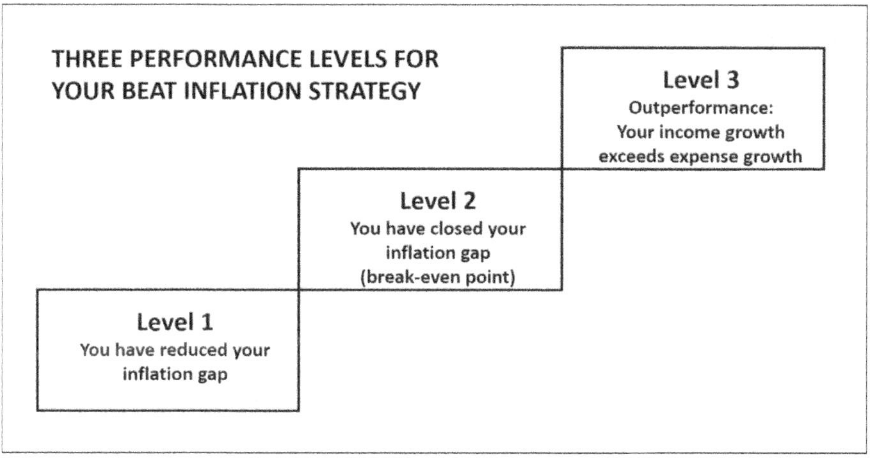

Reaching the first level is an important improvement and a step in the right direction. You closed part of your inflation gap either by raising your income level or by cutting your expenses (or both simultaneously). Getting to Level 1 should provide you with the motivational boost required to take you to the next level.

Level 2 is a real achievement and a milestone for your Beat Inflation game. Congratulations to those who achieve it. The measures you implemented fully eliminated your inflation gap. Income and expenses grow at the same rate leaving you in the desired world of being inflation-neutral. You defended your pre-inflation living standards against the vicious inflation dragon. In past inflation cycles, most people failed to accomplish this outcome (however, they did not have any guidance on how to manage inflation).

You should share your inflation-beating expertise with others. Let us help each other get to this level.

Level 3 is the "black belt" level. People who have achieved this level are true inflation-fighting champions. They managed to turn inflation risks into an opportunity and achieved the ideal outcome: Income grows faster than their expenses leading to real wealth creation.

People reaching Level 3 improve their standard of living. If you are among the lucky ones reaching this level, please make yourself available as a consultant to others. Your expertise is in great demand. Share your knowledge and expertise with your friends and family and with the broader public on social media.

Accept the fact that beating inflation is a significant challenge and that it will take time to see meaningful improvements. It will likely be a few weeks until you see the first positive results. Keep in mind that expense reductions will have an immediate impact on your financial bottom line. Increasing your income levels may take a little more time. Achieving meaningful income increases in your job or through side activities (e.g., passive income opportunities) may quickly change your inflation situation for the better. But you need patience to get to this point.

While you should prioritize your efforts on big opportunities, be reminded that many small improvements also have a significant impact on closing the inflation gap. Because small opportunities are sometimes easier to exploit than large ones, you should pursue any improvement, big or small, that is worthwhile.

The rules of this game are flexible and can be adapted to the needs of your team. The game is played to your benefit. Adjust any parameters to your liking. The most important point is to make progress on closing the inflation gap.

LINK UP WITH OTHER TEAMS TO CREATE A BEAT INFLATION MOVEMENT

Ideally, I would like to see Beat Inflation teams link up with each other locally, regionally, nationally, even internationally. Social media is an ideal platform to do so.

The first step to create momentum in this movement is to encourage other people to build their own Beat Inflation teams. Perhaps if you recommend this book to others or give them a short summary of what we are trying to accomplish, they may start their own groups and the movement gets bigger.

Second, reach out to other Beat Inflation teams to post questions and share experiences. I am currently exploring options on how to establish a Beat Inflation platform on social media. The goal is to have an intense and mutually beneficial exchange among all Beat Inflation teams.

CREATE AN INTERNATIONAL BEAT INFLATION MOVEMENT

My biggest goal is to create an international movement for this activity so that Beat Inflation teams can communicate with each other around the world. I believe that international exchanges can create an additional flow of ideas that would otherwise not be available to people.

These new international relationships could provide new opportunities. You could buy some of your needed supplies abroad. You might find a more cost-efficient education opportunity for your children abroad. You may learn from different types of thinking and problem-solving practices in different countries. As other countries may be further along in the inflation cycle, communicating with Beat Inflation teams in those countries may help you secure important insights and experiences.

At a minimum, you would make new international friends, learn about different cultures, and observe different ways of thinking about life experiences.

CHAPTER 5: THE DOUBLE VICTORY BEAT INFLATION PROGRAM

The DVBI program is a framework that will help you organize, structure, and plan your Beat Inflation activities. The program is a systematic approach seeking to achieve maximum success. It is structured like a pyramid, with four core activities.

In this chapter, I will describe the DBVI program in its entirety to give you an overview of the activities that will follow. Understanding the program in its entirety is important to avoid confusion and to facilitate implementation. Each of the following chapters will discuss one core activity.

Unfortunately, there will be some repetition from time to time. However, this is necessary to ensure a smooth top-down implementation of the program. Chart 19 shows the pyramid structure of the program.

Chart 19: Pyramid Structure of the DVBI Program

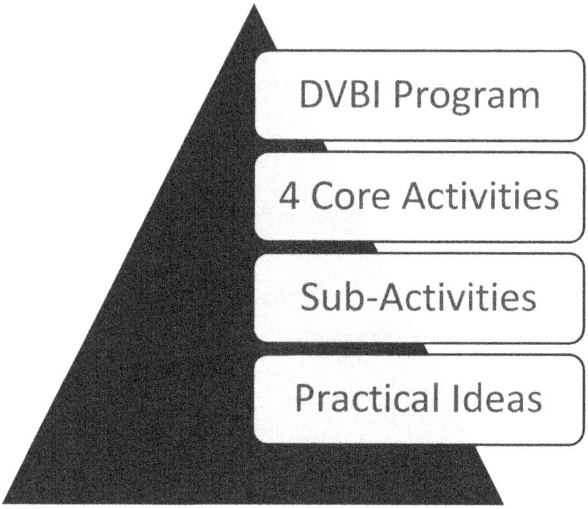

"Double Victory" stands for two objectives:

1. In the short term, the program is predominantly focused on supporting you in your fight with inflation. The four core activities and numerous individual ideas will be presented to help you face this enormous challenge.
2. In the long term, the program is designed to make you more successful, fulfilled, and happier. These core activities will also help us to become more productive, efficient, and effective. You should continue with this program regardless of the respective inflation situation. Seek continuous improvements for all four core activities and make the program a permanent part of your personal growth agenda.

Each core activity consists of many sub-activities and ideas to close the inflation gap. While these activities have the same purpose (i.e., beat inflation), they approach the problem from different angles and perspectives to maximize results. Chart 20 summarizes the main activities of the DVBI program.

Chart 20: The Double Victory Beat Inflation Program – Four Core Activities

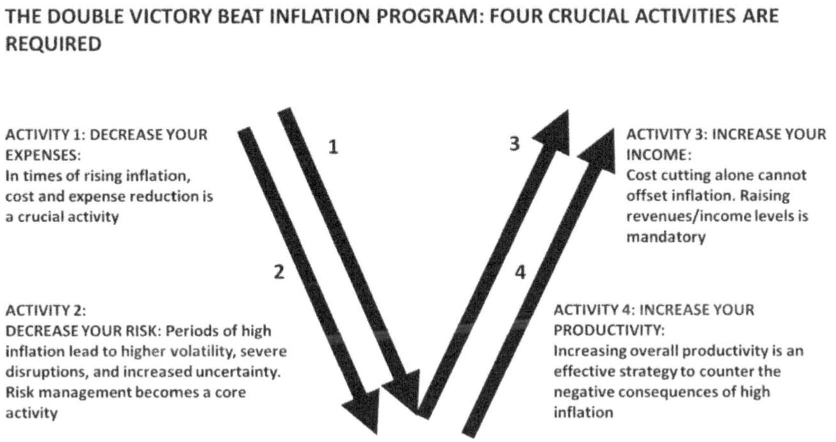

Looking at Chart 20 explains the name of the program. The four core activities twice form the letter "V" (victory).

CORE ACTIVITY 1: DECREASE YOUR EXPENSES (CHAPTER 6)

The first core activity is concerned with cost cutting. This is the easiest and fastest way to close a substantial part of the inflation gap. While cost cutting on its own may not be sufficient to eliminate the inflation gap in its totality, it will give you quick wins, which should provide a motivational boost. Do not stop after the first quick wins have been achieved. Continue to implement the remaining activities to achieve maximum success.

Finding cost-cutting opportunities may be easier today than in the past. Decades of strong economic growth coupled with significant wealth creation through investments in financial markets may have made us a bit negligent with our own spending discipline. Now is a good opportunity to stop wasteful and unnecessary spending.

The main goal is to make this activity as painless as possible. You do not want to go from one extreme (i.e., wasteful spending) to another (i.e., excessive frugality). However, some of us may need to go significantly beyond our initial comfort level to deal with personal inflation risks.

Cost cutting is not always a negative activity. In some instances, it will turn out to be a liberating activity that can greatly improve our social lives and our mental well-being. We can then reallocate our time to more beneficial activities such as watching movies together as a family or organizing outdoor events.

Cutting wasteful spending should be a relatively easy task. Every family spends a substantial amount of money each year on products and services that are rarely used. These opportunities may look small in isolation (e.g., a subscription to a magazine or media streaming service, impulse purchases of clothes, toys, or candy), but their aggregated costs can be significant. Forgoing purchases of no or low value are easy ways to cut your monthly expenses.

Eliminating the need for conspicuous consumption and exiting the "show off your wealth" competition can also be quite liberating. We are not only saving money; we are eliminating a quite dysfunctional and unsocial activity. There is beauty in modesty, as many famous ancient Greek philosophers claimed. A simple life is often a good and a fun life, as Anselm Gruen, German Benedictine monk and management trainer, has stated repeatedly.[14]

In other words, cost cutting is not only financially beneficial, it has many other positive side effects. It can help to ground us and refocus on things in life that are important and that will add value to our future. It can

---

[14] Anselm Gruen, Facebook message, August 27, 2022 (in German).

create clarity in our thoughts that will positively influence our professional and social lives.

But this is only the beginning. In the next chapter, I will introduce you to a systematic approach that is similar to the approaches used by professional management consultants in the corporate world. I can assure you that systematic cost-cutting approaches almost always exceed a client's expectations.

Based on my consulting work with corporate clients, cutting costs by 10% to 30% is often a normal outcome.[15] Keep in mind, if large professional companies can cut costs at this scale, you should be able to find similar opportunities. The key is to have a systematic, pragmatic approach that analyzes all relevant costs. You need to employ critical and creative thinking to find new cost-cutting targets or new solutions that eliminate or reduce expenses.

CORE ACTIVITY 2: DECREASE YOUR RISK EXPOSURE (CHAPTER 7)

You may wonder why improving your risk management approach is one of the four core activities of the DVBI program. The answer is simple. There are four immediate improvements to be achieved through better risk management:

1. **All risks you take are potential costs:** Any risk exposure can turn into a material expense in the future. Therefore, taking unnecessary or unquantifiable risks needs to be avoided.
2. **A period of high inflation is a high-risk period leaving no room for unnecessary additional risk taking**: Taking unnecessary risks during a period of high inflation is a dangerous strategy. You are

[15] Based on the relevant cost base of a cost cutting project.

exposing yourself to risk events at a time when your risk absorption capacity is already strained or depleted. Therefore, it is important to eliminate risk-taking activities that are not mission critical for your life or are not accompanied by exceptional opportunities.

3. **Try to avoid unnecessary distraction:** Taking excessive risks can turn into a major distraction as fear and uncertainty capture your attention and motivation. Such distractions can have a negative impact on activities that should be pursued with the highest priority (e.g., implementing the DBVI program). High inflation periods require focus. As Confucius reportedly said: The man who chases two rabbits catches neither.

4. **Sophisticated risk management improves the quality of our decisions:** We can substantially improve the quality of our decisions if we incorporate risk management principles and considerations into the decision-making process. In fact, most of the problems we face today are caused by a simple failure: We ignored risk management considerations when we made important decisions in the past. The return of high inflation to modern society is an unfortunate example of failed risk management in the past. Even many large corporations failed to anticipate higher inflation when making strategic decisions in the past.

In Chapter 7, we will focus on the following risk topics in particular:

- Improving the quality of our decisions by including risk management considerations into the decision-making process
- Reducing health-related risks
- Improving our financial risk management
- Managing our location risk

In general, you should always strive for eliminating risks that are not clearly linked to a sizeable and meaningful opportunity. Otherwise, it constitutes a waste of your time and resources. Taking such risks are roadblocks for our ambition to close the inflation gap.

I should note that severe risk events may also present some attractive risk-taking opportunities. While this may sound paradoxical, it is true, and there is a simple explanation. When an unprepared society is hit by a substantial risk event, people tend to react with excessive emotionality. Many panic and make irrational decisions by using sections of their primitive brain (often referred to as the limbic system).

We witnessed this during the 1970s inflation crisis. After the unexpected arrival of high inflation in 1973, the stock market went from being substantially over-valued to substantially undervalued. At that time, people who approached the stock market in an unemotional and rational way exploited this phenomenal opportunity by buying cheap quality stocks. Warren Buffett increased the stock valuation of his company, Berkshire Hathaway, by about 900% during the 1970s inflation crisis.[16]

In principle, we should always look at the decisions we make by equally focusing on opportunities and associated risks. Unfortunately, most people over-focus on opportunities and neglect associated risks. Such an imbalance is dangerous. Although this may be advantageous in the short term, you are exposed to substantial risks in the future.

---

[16] I provide a more detailed discussion of Warren Buffett's investment strategy in my book *The Return of High Inflation*.

CORE ACTIVITY 3: INCREASE YOUR INCOME (CHAPTER 8)

For most people, closing the inflation gap requires more than just cost cutting. The challenge is simply too great to be fully addressed by reducing your cost base. Nor should people exclusively focus on cost cutting and spending discipline. This would leave one extremely powerful lever for improving our financial position untouched: raising our income level.

Focusing simultaneously on the two levers of cost containment and income expansion is a powerful strategy to improve your financial bottom line. Unfortunately, few people choose this path. My experience suggests that the vast majority focus on either cost containment or income expansion.

Before asking for a salary increase due to inflation, you need to make sure that you operate from a safe basis; that is, to ensure that your current job is secure. You need to be in good standing at your current employer.

The key question in this context is: Are you mission critical to your employer? If yes, you can ask for a substantial salary increase immediately. Those who are mission critical will not be fired in a recession. Your employer will be afraid of losing you and will try to accommodate you.

If you are not mission critical to your employer, you should change this immediately. Average or below average performers are not only at risk of not getting sufficient salary increases, they can quickly lose their jobs if their company's results weaken or a severe recession hits the economy. Chapter 8 will discuss strategies to make you mission critical to your employer.

There are three different strategies to expand your total income. Your current job is only one option. Let us look at three income-generating options (to be discussed in Chapter 8):

1. **Secure your current job**: You need to ensure that your current job is secure. Losing your salary through job loss is a major setback in your quest to beat inflation. Unfortunately, your job will never be completely secure. Your employer may experience a financial crisis and dismiss you through no fault of your own. Therefore, part of this activity is to have a Plan B in place (one or several job opportunities awaiting you – just in case).

   Increasing your job security in many cases will mean changing your perspective about work. It is not only a job anymore, but a profession that is important, that you are proud of doing, and that requires a different attitude, a higher level of engagement, and more discipline. Regardless of what level you occupy in your company, approaching your employment as a profession will do wonders. Supervisors will notice the change (clients/customers too) and new opportunities may arise.

   Keep in mind that having a secure job means that you are in one way or another mission critical to your employer. Now is the time to ask for salary increases and promotions.

2. **Negotiate sufficient salary increases to beat inflation:** One of the most important activities to beat inflation is to ask for salary increases that offset inflation. Initially, this might be a struggle. However, with the right strategy you may not only accomplish this goal, you might even succeed in raising your salary level beyond actual inflation rates. The key for achieving this goal is to leverage your importance to your employer. Becoming mission critical provides you with the required amount of bargaining power. Being afraid of losing you to a competitor, your employer will strive to keep you within the organization. You will achieve mission-critical status by improving your work attitude, upgrading your skill portfolio, and asking for and accepting more job-related responsibilities.

3. **Exploit additional income-generating opportunities (outside your current job):** The third string of activities is concerned with finding

and exploiting additional income-generating opportunities outside your main employment. There is a wide spectrum of possibilities available to you (and your family members) to accomplish this. The easiest and most traditional opportunity is to get an extra job to supplement your current salary.

While this will help close your inflation gap, working an extra job can put a lot of strain on your health, family, and social life. The key is to find a job that is both rewarding and manageable (e.g., a person with solid math knowledge may offer math tutoring to students).

The more exciting opportunities to generate extra income, however, are those that exploit opportunities created by modern technology. Digitization has opened up a new world of attractive income opportunities to the general public (e.g., creating an online tutorial and selling it on one of the many course platforms for online learning). There are numerous ways available to pursue passive income opportunities. The attractive feature is the scalability of your business model. For example, an initial time investment to create an online course can create an attractive income stream that may last for years and does not need significant additional time investments.

Chapter 8 will present a systematic approach to secure existing income and to exploit new income opportunities. The amount of additional income available to people is usually beyond their most optimistic expectations. In that sense, the DVBI program will present opportunities that go significantly beyond the initial goal of closing the inflation gap and may change your life for the better. For some, an initial activity aimed at generating additional income will turn into an attractive business opportunity. You may awaken one day to life as an entrepreneur.

CORE ACTIVITY 4: INCREASE YOUR PRODUCTIVITY

The last core activity focuses on raising your overall productivity. This activity may have the most profound impact on your life and future success.

Our main concerns are time allocation and productivity. The latter measures the output per unit of time invested. Getting more done within a given unit of time will free up time that can be used for other activities. In the context of this book, we will use a large part of this extra time to implement the DVBI program.

The DVBI program may require significant extra work and time. This extra time should not exclusively come from curtailing your free time. You should engage in productivity-boosting activities to free up time from other activities. Getting things done faster or eliminating low/no value activities will allow you to draw from this extra time bucket to execute activities required to fight inflation risks. Ideally, you will also free up extra time for your family, friends, and hobbies. People who have successfully improved their productivity are always amazed at the results. They achieve more in less time and have a balanced life.

The starting point will be an analysis of your current use of time, its allocation to different activity buckets, and the achieved output. Using your time wisely is an important priority. The great Roman philosopher Seneca provides some valuable insights on time management in his essay, "On the Shortness of Life." Even though written about 2000 years ago, I recommend this as one of the best time management books available to this date.

According to Seneca, time is more important than money. Money lost in a business transaction can be regained. A unit of time wasted on a trivial activity is lost forever. It is a permanent loss. This view of time as a limited and extremely valuable resource should guide our approach to time management (as described in Chapter 9).

Chapter 9 provides a crash course in improving productivity, a powerful tool for combatting both inflation and underperformance issues. Although you should pay significant attention to time management and self-organization, you should also focus on a productive use of the assets you own. For example, an unused garage can be transformed into a work area or rented out to third parties. In this case, you increase the productivity of an asset you own. A garden can be used to grow fruits and vegetables. In this case you increase the productivity of your garden.

The same way managers in the corporate world are constantly looking for opportunities to raise productivity, you should continue to diligently search for productivity-raising opportunities in your life. It will make you a more successful, fulfilled, and happier person. The number of available opportunities is unlimited. You just have to find and exploit them.

In conclusion, the four core activities of the DVBI program consist of easy-to-implement action steps designed to eliminate the inflation gap and make you more successful. They have the potential to catapult you to a higher performance level, an outcome that goes beyond the original goal of beating inflation.

The recommended team approach should lead to faster improvements and better results. It also provides you with motivation and emotional support along the way. Therefore, start building your Beat Inflation team as soon as possible.

CHAPTER 6: DECREASE YOUR EXPENSES (CORE ACTIVITY #1)

Introductory comments:

The DVBI program starts with the easiest target: reducing our expenses. Almost immediately, we will find ways to cut our spending and renegotiate our financial commitments. Cutting our expenses lets us win twice: First, we save money, and second, we can invest the saved amount and earn a return on it over time.

In this chapter, we will pursue the following two victories:

***Victory 1 (short-term inflation focus):** Cost cutting is an important activity to close the inflation gap. It may not be sufficient, but it will get us started quite quickly. The program has elements similar to those I use when working as a management consultant with large corporations. It is systematic and leaves no stone unturned. It consists of ten sub-activities containing many practical ideas and suggestions. Don't wait. Let's get started. Save money by cutting unneeded expenses!*

***Victory 2 (long-term personal growth):** There is more to cost cutting than just reducing our expenses. We want to approach it as a liberating activity that gets us focused on the important things in life. Often, a simple life is also a happier life. Let us impress other people with our personality and character and not with expensive designer brands. Buying items that we do not need distracts us from our important goals. Subscribing to media streaming services leads to a passive lifestyle that is bad for our health. Let us save money for when we really need it (e.g., retirement, children's education, real fun activities, emergencies). We will feel happier when we spend less.*

The goal of the first core activity is to significantly reduce our expenses and costs without inflicting excessive pain and sacrifice. Reducing our overall spending is one of the most important activities during a period of high inflation. While activities geared at raising our income level need time to bear fruit, cost-cutting activities work immediately.

Keep in mind that every dollar you save from reducing expenses can be invested in a safe asset class to increase your income (e.g., interest income). Therefore**, cost cutting rewards you twice.**

Unfortunately, people tend to procrastinate cost-cutting activities until a deteriorating financial situation forces them to do so. Once signs of financial stress appear, you have waited too long and wasted valuable time and money. Therefore, our commitment to sophisticated cost-cutting practices should remain in place even if high inflation ceases to be an immediate threat.

The good news is that reducing our expenses is not only easy to do but can be done in a way that minimizes its overall impact. In most cases, we do not have to shut down our social life or eliminate all enjoyable activities or hobbies. There are "easy win" cost-cutting activities available to most of us that do not negatively impact our social life and overall happiness.

For example, we often spend money on items we do not use (e.g., subscriptions to magazines, internet or social media streaming services, unnecessary insurance policies, clothing, food). Eliminating such waste of our financial resources is a good way to start this exercise.

Advice from ancient Greek philosophy:

Epicurus (341-270 BC) was an ancient Greek philosopher who developed a philosophy of living a happy life (Epicureanism). One key recommendation was to reduce our needs, wants, and desires. This would make us instantly richer (as we spend less and have more money left) and happier. Once we have adopted a simple life, an occasional luxury item creates much more joy and happiness than before. There is a lot of wisdom in this thought. Try it.

Hence, cutting our spending can be a liberating activity that leads to more fulfillment and happiness.

Cost cutting does not have to be a boring "number-crunching" activity. It can be a fun social event. You can meet with friends and share ideas and experiences, perhaps even set up a competition and reward those with the most valuable ideas.

A great idea is to include your children in this activity, thus teaching them basic financial management skills. You may even reward them for expense reductions they suggest or help exploit by sharing a part of the overall savings with them.

There are many ways children can be included in your cost-cutting initiative:

- Conduct internet research to find cheaper prices for products and services you regularly consume. You will be amazed how quickly they find better prices from vendors on the internet.
- Perform chores for which you hire external help (e.g., cleaning, gardening, repairing simple products, painting a house, washing a car).
- Reduce their own spending (e.g., choose cheaper brands, buy used products). Again, you may offer a small reward in exchange.

- Generate new income opportunities (e.g., organize a garage sale, sell products you do not need any more on the internet).

The key is to organize the activity as a competitive game, transfer responsibilities to them, and resist the temptation to micromanage. Give your children the freedom they need to develop their own ideas. Let them prove themselves to you.

One idea for people in the U.S. (or other countries with high educational expenses):

For most families, the biggest cost item is their children's education. This is particularly true in the United States. To address this issue, incentivize your children to obtain a merit-based scholarship at a reputable university.

First, reward your child (financially or otherwise) for good grades, extra effort, and academic awards even at a young age. Your child will learn to view school as a job that pays well (based on extra effort) and not as a mandatory boring activity meant to please others.

Second, most children do not comprehend the enormous financial resources required to attend college. What they do understand are financial rewards, particularly if they have a part-time job and realize what hard work means. As your children get older, offer them a share of the college cost savings if they obtain a merit scholarship. By doing so you create a win-win situation. Parents will reduce their educational expenses and children will appreciate the monetary reward.

This strategy may be one of your biggest cost-cutting successes.

HOW TO START

To make your cost-cutting effort successful, you need to create some structure. It is important to systematically screen your spending habits and quickly find the issues that require corrective action.

The first activity should be focused on creating cost transparency. Very often, people do not understand their own expense structure and, more importantly, how it compares to other people's spending patterns.

Therefore, we need to first create transparency on our spending and expenses. An easy way to do this is to create a yearly and monthly overview of our spending by category. This is not an academic exercise. Feel free to use round amounts or estimates when you are missing exact numbers. Since a large share of transactions are facilitated by credit cards, card statements can be a tremendous help for this analysis. Most credit card companies provide free annual analysis of your spending history organized by helpful categories.

You are then ready to take action and start saving money.

Our cost-cutting activities should fulfill the following four requirements (see Chart 21).

Chart 21: Requirements for Cost-Cutting Activities

Best Practice Cost-Cutting – Key Requirements
1. SYSTEMATIC: Analyze your cost structure systematically to ensure no relevant opportunity will be missed. 2. STRUCTURED: Follow a structured approach that helps increase efficiency and effectiveness. 3. FOCUSED: Focus on activities that have the highest cost-cutting potential. 4. PRIORITIZED: Prioritize initiatives by size, ease of execution, and timing.

If possible, obtain data for previous years to compare spending patterns, which may help you identify additional cost-cutting opportunities. For example, identifying a pattern of eating out more often or in expensive restaurants could be a starting point for immediate corrective action (e.g., choose cheaper restaurants, eat out less often).

Chart 22 lists ten cost-cutting initiatives that are part of the DVBI program. Feel free to add any additional initiatives you may feel are worthwhile. Please keep in mind that many small activities can add up to significant savings. Often, such small activities can be implemented within minutes (e.g., cancel a paid subscription to a service you do not use).

Chart 22: Ten Cost-Cutting Initiatives

Number	Initiative	Status
1	Eliminate no-value-added expenses	
2	Reduce the frequency of spending or the amount spent on an item	
3	Change your purchasing habits	
4	Find cheaper substitutes	
5	Employ self-sufficiency strategies	
6	(Re)negotiate prices or terms for all purchases	
7	Avoid unnecessary complexity that leads to higher expenses in the future	
8	Avoid boomerang costs	
9	Compare your own spending with that of relatives, friends, and colleagues (benchmarking)	
10	Find high impact, best-practice examples employed by others and copy them (survey your friends)	

To track your progress, include an estimated completion date in the "Status" column.

#1: ELIMINATE NO-VALUE-ADDED EXPENSES

Most of us occasionally spend money on products or services that provide very little value to our lives or our strategic goals. These purchases are made on an impulse. We do not critically reflect on them at the time of purchase. However, they can add up significantly over time. For example, purchasing a candy bar or magazine while waiting in line at a cash register in a supermarket (remember, these items are put there on purpose) or purchasing an item advertised on TV through an infomercial.

Even worse, such purchases can lead to value destruction for us or our family members (e.g., excessive amounts of unhealthy junk food, subscriptions to streaming services that prevent us from using our time more wisely).

Now is the time to end such wasteful spending. Going forward, whenever you make a purchase or place an order on an impulse, ask yourself what value this transaction creates for you or your family. If you make this a routine, you will quickly save a large amount of money without negatively impacting your happiness. A typical quick win.

PERSONAL EXAMPLE:

I have practically eliminated sugar consumption from my daily eating habits. Since it may sometimes be difficult to find healthy food while travelling, I made it a habit to bring my own food. A great way to save money as well.

When I took my family to an amusement park, I brought a refillable water bottle and some fruits and sandwiches for the day in my backpack. When waiting in line for one of the rides, I could not help notice how much other families spent on unhealthy, overpriced food and snacks. A quick math calculation suggests that families easily spend about $200 for unhealthy food and snacks in amusement parks (assuming a five-day period). This represents a big opportunity for cutting costs.

Let us approach this topic with a different activity. Take a look at the documents you prepared for creating cost transparency (monthly credit card statements, annual credit card spending analysis, manually prepared list of other spending via cash or bank transfer). Go through these documents and circle all transactions that neither created value nor increased your happiness in a meaningful and lasting way.

Be prepared to watch out for the following:

- **Unnecessary insurance policies:** While some policies may add little value given their cost (e.g., extended warranties on inexpensive items), others provide double coverage; that is, you pay for covering a risk that is already covered by a different policy you have. Few people know that their credit cards often include valuable insurance coverages for free (e.g., for car rentals, theft, accident insurance, travel insurance). Additionally, memberships in certain associations or interest groups often include a bundle of insurance services. Please check the fine print or call the respective company for more information.

- **Unhealthy food or drink products.**
- **Toys for children** that will be used only for a short amount of time.
- **Toys for children** that have a negative impact on their development (e.g., video gaming equipment) and may lead to additional costs in the future (e.g., tutoring if school performance deteriorates).
- **Subscriptions** to magazines you do not read or media services you rarely use (or can easily do without).
- **Items** often **bought on impulse** (e.g., purchases at a cash register in a supermarket, items purchased in a mall). Be careful about purchases initiated by TV or internet commercials. Have a "one more day" policy in place. You wait one day before you purchase to determine whether you still consider the product to have value. You will be surprised how often you will change your mind about a purchase after a day of reflection.
- **Add-on products:** You may be offered additional products at a discount to your purchase. For example, when you buy a pair of new shoes you may be offered a second pair for half the price. If you don't need an extra pair of shoes, don't buy them. "Fake" discounts: You may be offered a quantity discount to incentivize you to buy more items than you originally planned (e.g., a price reduction of 10 percent if you buy five items or more). Again, if you don't need the additional items, do not buy them. Some people mistakenly see unused discounts or coupons as a waste of money. However, it is a true waste of money if you buy items you do not need.
- **Annual fees** for credit cards you do not use anymore.
- **Check return policies** for low-value items that you purchased recently. Can you still return them? Can you sell them online?

#2: REDUCE THE FREQUENCY OF SPENDING OR THE AMOUNT SPENT ON AN ITEM

There are many cost-cutting opportunities available that do not require a radical lifestyle change or significant reduction of your social activities. All that is needed is a little moderation. In other words, reduce your spending without eliminating or excessively curtailing your (social) activities. Just make moderation a part of your set of values.

> Stoic philosophers always considered **moderation** an important virtue to obtain happiness. A modest life is a simpler life enabling us to pursue activities that create real and long-lasting happiness. Roman emperor and Stoic philosopher Marcus Aurelius mastered the minimalist practice of moderation. It is reported that he declined having a bed and preferred instead sleeping on the floor. Admittedly, an extreme example.
>
> Even if you do not copy this practice, experiment with making moderation a part of your life routines. It may dramatically reduce your expenses.

As Chart 23 shows, achieving cost reductions through moderation can be done through four different approaches.

Chart 23: Cost Cutting through Moderation

No.	Approach
1	**Reduce frequency of an expense:** Slightly reduce the frequency of an activity or purchase.
2	**Downgrade:** Choose a cheaper category or brand.
3	**Skip:** Skip (low value) features or elements of an activity or purchase.
4	**Delay:** Delay your purchase, as you may be able to obtain a discount in the future, particularly if a new model is released in the meantime.

Ways to practice moderation include:

- **Purchase of electronics (e.g., smartphone, laptop, TV):** Extend your normal replacement cycle by a year or more. Choose a version that is one notch below your current model or choose last year's model at a discount.
- **Car purchase:** Cars typically lose much of their value during the first three years. Therefore, extending the use of your car beyond three years may be beneficial (unless you lease your car). Choose a model or equipment package that is slightly below the ranking of your current model or your originally planned purchase.
- **Restaurant visits:** It is astonishing how much money you can save on this cost category without noticing any significant sacrifice. Reduce the frequency of your dining out activities by a small amount. Choose a restaurant that is one category below your usual choice. Skip (or share) one item on your order (appetizer or dessert). My health choice to skip dessert has saved me a lot of money over the years and has contributed to better health.

  Dine out at less expensive times (e.g., happy hours, special discount times, lunch instead of dinner). Reduce the number and/or quality of drinks (choose a house wine over a more expensive brand).

- **Choose cheaper seats (e.g., cinema, theater, sporting events):** Purchase cheaper seats than you did in the past (e.g., sit a little bit more in the back) or choose a performance that is cheaper (e.g., matinee versus evening event).
- **Vacation spending:** Choose a slightly lower rated hotel or a smaller room. Select a lower category for your rental car or a lower class/cheaper airline ticket. If possible, book your vacation during off-seasons, as this can lead to substantial savings.
- **Other purchases:** When buying items such as clothes or shoes, choose a brand that is slightly below the price category of your typical preferences. Consider postponing your purchase to receive an off-season discount.

Practicing moderation may generate significant cost savings. You will be amazed when you implement this strategy. It also gets you and your family more grounded, recognizing that there is more to life than "spend to impress" strategies.

#3: CHANGE YOUR PURCHASING HABITS

Large professional companies run central purchasing departments to lower the cost of products and materials they need by using the following strategies (Chart 24):

Chart 24: Strategies Used by Corporate Purchasing Departments

Professional Purchasing Strategies
1. Pooling orders across business units to demand bulk discounts. 2. Following seasonal pricing patterns to reduce purchasing costs. 3. Increasing inventories to take advantage of rising prices (during times of high inflation).

The good news is that these strategies are also available to you. You just have to change your purchasing habits.

To qualify for a bulk discount, buy less frequently but in larger quantities. You can also pool orders with relatives, neighbors, and friends. Vendors often offer additional discounts for very large orders.

Leveraging seasonal pricing trends is the second strategy you may adopt. For example, as a student and young professional I always bought my ski equipment and clothes at the end of a season. While I had to wait until the next winter to use the equipment, I regularly received discounts between 50% and 75%. There is another positive side to post-season buying activities. You beat the price increases that typically occur between last season's prices and those of the new season due to inflation. This difference can be quite high during times of high inflation.

The third strategy is particularly interesting. At the time this book was written, bank interest rates on checking accounts were still very low, while inflation in the United States (and in many other countries) crossed the 8% mark. To take advantage of this disconnect, you may substantially increase your home inventory of non-perishable items that you will use over the next two years, particularly those that are on sale. Think of it this way: If your money does not earn any interest, you may as well "invest" it in non-perishable and easy-to-store items you regularly use. You save the price increases that would occur over the next one to two years.

Items that qualify for "prebuying" include:

- Food that comes in cans or dried forms (e.g., rice, pasta, beans, coffee)
- Cleaning products
- Personal hygiene products (e.g., soap)
- Spare parts that are regularly needed (e.g., AC filters, light bulbs, water filters, print cartridges)
- Fitness equipment that needs frequent replacement (e.g., running shoes)
- Garden equipment

Maintaining a higher inventory level has another positive side effect. Periods of high inflation often lead to supply chain disruptions and product unavailability. This strategy protects you from such disruptions. You may even sell some of your own inventory at a profit during such disruptive periods.

Another strategy is to negotiate bulk discounts for qualifying purchases. Pool your purchases with other people (e.g., friends, colleagues, relatives, members of your Beat Inflation team) to increase your bargaining power. This strategy works across very different product and service categories. Here are a few examples:

- Schedule landscaping, roof repair, driveway refinishing, tree-cutting work as a group of neighbors
- Obtain group membership in a wholesale shopping venue
- Schedule group appointments for special hair treatments (e.g., expensive coloring)
- Purchase house or garden furniture or equipment as a group ("create big orders")
- Obtain group membership in fitness centers or country clubs
- Purchase group tickets for sports, entertainment, and cultural events

#4: FIND CHEAPER SUBSTITUTES

Periods of high inflation can lead to erratic price movements for some items. Often, this is driven by isolated and temporary supply chain disruptions or other irregular patterns.

Finding a cheaper substitute for products we use regularly is an effective way to cut costs. Often, switching to lower cost substitutes does not have any impact on our life. There is little or no sacrifice involved.

In principle, there are four different strategies available to you (see Chart 25).

Chart 25: Finding and Using Substitute Products

Using Substitute Products

1. Opportunistic switching
2. Switch to a cheaper brand
3. Use products with a lower but still acceptable quality ranking
4. Replace with different products offering similar utility

Opportunistic switching among similar product categories can help avoid such price peaks. For example, you may switch among different forms of grains, legumes, and fruit.

You can choose cheaper brands or downgrade your brand preferences to those more affordable. Often, no-brand products or house brands offered by grocery chains are of similar or at least acceptable quality while being significantly cheaper.

You may also consider moving down the "quality spectrum" of a product. For example, you may switch to non-organic foods, purchase the paperback or electronic version of a book instead of a more expensive hardcopy, buy a used book or borrow the book from a library.

The goal is to sacrifice a quality feature that is not essential to you and your most important needs in order to achieve substantial cost savings. Do not employ this strategy, however, if it exposes you to additional, potentially significant, new risks. For example, buying an unstable, low-quality ladder just to save money is not advisable. Never compromise on safety and health issues.

Finally, you can switch to a different product to fulfill a similar requirement. A good example is to purchase plant protein over meat protein. In many cases, such a (temporary) switch can lead to significant cost savings (if your medical situation allows doing so), especially if you prepare meals from scratch.

There are many additional ideas for implementing this strategy:

- Switching from an expensive sport (e.g., golf) to a less expensive one (e.g., running, hiking)
- Switching from an expensive hobby (e.g., wine tasting) to a cheaper one (e.g., reading)

- Switching from an expensive country club membership to a much less expensive one or joining a group of people interested in similar activities without committing to a costly membership

When you study dramatic events in history, you find many additional examples. During World War II, regular coffee was either not available in Germany or was outrageously expensive. Some clever people created a cheap substitute product based on a combination of barley, malted barley, chicory, and rye. While the alternative did not offer the caffeine, it came close in taste and appearance to the original product. Interestingly, during the 1990s this coffee substitute was relaunched in Germany and is now marketed to young health-conscious urban professionals. This turned out to be a smart business idea.

It may make sense to interview people who have experienced periods of hardship in their lives. They may have a list of strategies available that they employed during such times to substitute regular products with cheaper alternatives. You may not only learn a few ideas on how to save money, but also come up with a new business idea. You can also post questions on social media sites to generate new ideas. Be creative and inquisitive. Ask many questions.

#5: EMPLOY SELF-SUFFICIENCY STRATEGIES

It is very likely that this strategy was extensively used by your parents or grandparents decades ago. Practicing full or partial self-sufficiency is a fun and fulfilling way to save a substantial amount of money while doing something good. The underlying idea is simple: Perform the job that third-party vendors do for you.

There are four different categories of self-sufficiency strategies:

1. **Grow your own food:** Maintaining your own garden is a financially and emotionally rewarding activity. The key is to choose produce that fits your personal situation and is compatible with the available space, soil conditions, your time availability, your gardening experience, and the climate of your region. Also, you may initially focus on low maintenance gardening to keep your motivation high. For example, you may grow fruit trees and then exchange your produce with others (e.g., your apples for your neighbor's plums) or grow herbs and vegetables in containers or on small patches of soil. Not surprisingly, growing your own food can quickly become a substantial money saver. It is also a rewarding activity for the whole family.

   Unfortunately, we have been neglecting this rewarding activity. This is also a pity for our children's development as they lack such important experiences. When inflation hit Germany during the 1970s, my family was spared from food price inflation, since most of our vegetables, legumes, fruit, salads, and herbs came directly from our garden. Unknowingly, when my grandparents bought our garden, they also created a powerful inflation hedge.

2. **Build/create things yourself:** There is a wide spectrum of items that we do not need to buy in stores. We can build them ourselves and save a substantial amount of money. Obviously, experience and training play a big role in determining the building activities that can be assumed safely. Some ideas include:
   i. Build simple pieces of furniture (e.g., shelves).
   ii. Create or print your own greeting cards (e.g., for holiday seasons, birthdays).
   iii. Create your own home or party decorations (e.g., wall hangings, place settings).
   iv. Build your own toys and play items for children (one of my friends built a zip line and a tree house for his children). More simple activities work as well.

v. Build window screens (custom-made window screens often cost 20 times the price of the materials needed to build your own screens).

3. **Repair/maintain items yourself:** High inflation will add to already high prices for repairing items you own. Often, there is a chance to save a substantial amount of money by taking on simple, but time-intensive (and therefore expensive) repair or maintenance tasks. Videos on social media often provide excellent tutorials to help us repair things quickly.

   In addition to cost savings, there can be a significant time advantage if you do not have to wait for the arrival of professional repair staff. It can be a rewarding experience to successfully fix items you would have replaced with new purchases in the past. Also, you are contributing to saving the planet by avoiding additional waste creation.

4. **Do it yourself:** There are many tasks that you can do yourself without hiring expensive professionals:
   i. Do your own landscaping (e.g., cut lawn, trim hedges, cut tree branches on smaller trees).
   ii. Wash your own car.
   iii. Paint your house or interior rooms.
   iv. Cut each other's hair (during the COVID pandemic, many people achieved a sufficient skill level).

#6: (RE)NEGOTIATE PRICES OR TERMS FOR ALL PURCHASES

I know people who literally never purchase an item without trying to negotiate a better price, whether it be for clothes, books, ice cream from a street vendor, or groceries. Price negotiation is in their DNA. They simply ask for a discount on all their purchases. I am always amazed at how often they succeed in achieving a price reduction. Sometimes the discount is small, sometimes big. The point is that their consistency results in huge cost savings over time.

Sometimes there is a reason why they ask for a discount (a product may have a slight fault or the packaging might be damaged), but often there is not. They do the same with maintenance contracts and other ongoing expenses.

This strategy comes with an incredible track record. Impressive cost savings can be achieved just by making such a request. It is simple, but few people do so consistently.

Those who do follow this strategy also improve their negotiation skills over time. There is a steep learning curve and making progress can be very rewarding. Becoming a good negotiator may also help you in other aspects of life.

During periods of high inflation, we need to adopt this strategy. High inflation brings price volatility and uncertainty. Even retail vendors do not know what the "right" price is, as they do not know whether their suppliers will deliver ordered products in time or whether they will run low in inventory. Nor do they know what future prices for replacement orders will be or when new inventory will arrive.

Therefore, many vendors and stores follow a simple strategy when setting prices during periods of high inflation: they err on the upside, knowing that the majority of people act as price-takers; that is, they do not make a serious effort to negotiate prices. As few customers make this effort, it is easy for vendors to grant concessions to a small group of people, when most people pay full price.

When I travelled to countries with high inflation in the past, I was amazed by how arbitrarily prices were set and how non-binding they were. In some cases, just my hesitation to complete a transaction was interpreted by a vendor as an act of negotiation and led to a price reduction.

We must remember that prices are subjectively set to capture the maximum amount of revenue from people who do not negotiate. Prices are rarely absolute or final. Therefore, starting a negotiation process should be a logical step to protect our financial wealth. Many vendors enjoy attractive profit margins that leave room for lowering a price without sacrificing a still attractive profit on a discounted transaction. Make negotiating a habit not only during periods of inflation but also after inflation has been contained.

Let us review some ideas for (re-)negotiating prices:

- **Subscriptions to newspapers and magazines:** When I did not renew my subscription to a financial magazine, I was immediately offered a 50% discount without even making such a request (I simply forgot to renew).
- **Subscriptions to any form of services:** Any type of service agreement can be negotiated. This includes cable television services, internet services, streaming services, and delivery services.
- **Purchase of large appliances and consumer electronics.**
- **Buying or leasing a car:** It is very easy to find out the actual sales price for almost all standard cars in your region on the internet. This price transparency gives you a great advantage for your negotiation.
- **Using coupons:** Searching for coupons on the internet is often a good strategy. But even if you do not find a coupon, there is hope for a discount. Ask the sales staff for available coupons. Sales personnel often guide you to available coupons on the internet that you did not find, particularly if they receive a commission on the sale amount they generate. Some sales people have a stack of coupons available that they will use if asked.
- **Slow down the sales process:** There is nothing that sales people dislike more than people who take a long time to decide. Therefore, slow down the sales process by asking many questions. Make phone calls to friends to discuss prices. Sales personnel are eager to make the deal and to move to the next customer. Therefore, they may be willing to offer extra discounts to speed up the transaction.

Again, just make it a routine to ask for a discount whenever you make a purchase. Doing so may create substantial savings over time.

#7: AVOID UNNECESSARY COMPLEXITY THAT LEADS TO HIGHER EXPENSES IN THE FUTURE

"Simplicity wins" is a common slogan in management literature. What is mostly true for professional companies is also true for your personal life. Reducing complexity is not only a mentally liberating and mood-lifting activity, it also can substantially reduce your current and future spending. In addition, avoiding complexity prevents you from losing valuable time in the future.

One example of a true "complexity monster" is overly integrated technology. In so-called "smart houses," all mechanical, electrical, technological, and thermic devices are now integrated into one monolithic system. You can control literally everything in your house with one "super app" on your smart phone (e.g., lifting the blinds, starting the lawn sprinklers, setting the temperature, checking the alarm system, reviewing the contents of your refrigerator).

Here comes the inflation catch. In the beginning, these systems will work fine and they can make life much easier. However, after a few years, malfunctioning issues will occur and they will increase in frequency. Due to the complexity of the system, you may need to hire expensive experts to diagnose and fix the problems. Unfortunately, with rising inflation the costs for maintaining these systems and fixing malfunctions can increase substantially over time. It can also be quite frustrating when there is a problem and there is no expert available to help you.

Eventually, your smart house solution will be as outdated as your smart phone. You will then face a significant choice: upgrade or migrate to a new system. Chart 26 summarizes the three phases that apply to all complex systems.

Chart 26: The Three Phases of an Overly Complex System

Phase	Description	Cost Impact
1	Introduction • Initial implementation • Short period of multiple "bugs" appearing, which are typically fixed free of charge	High (initial purchase) Low (for maintenance)
2	Short period of proper functioning ("excitement") • System works as intended • Often, this period is relatively short (2-3 years) • No need for extensive repairs or maintenance	Low-medium
3	Aging of system ("frustration") • Number of malfunctions increases at an accelerating rate • Frequent (expensive) repairs by highly paid experts needed • Expensive replacement (upgrade of system or migration to new platform) is needed	(Extremely) high, impacted by inflation

One of the key problems of complex systems is that associated costs occur with a time lag. This makes complex systems so dangerous during periods of high inflation. Repair and replacement costs become much higher than originally planned.

The problem with highly integrated systems is that it is costly to diagnose the cause of a fault. Since complex systems cannot be fixed by yourself or a cost-effective handyman, you need to hire a highly paid expert. You will eventually reach the point where a total replacement and re-configuration is necessary. Complexity monsters are one area where inflation "bites" the most.

> If you want to keep future spending low, avoid complexity. Prefer simple solutions wherever possible. Think twice when offered to integrate multiple activities into one system. You may opt for modern solutions, but resist the temptation to fully integrate all systems into one central "super system."

Excessive complexity can be found everywhere around us. In fact, modern society excels at making simple things overly complex. Examples include:

- Smart cars are packed with complex computer systems that are overly integrated into "super systems." They include sensitive and often hard to fix devices (e.g., sensors, motorized equipment). Aging of these components becomes a real problem as repairs become difficult to perform and spare parts difficult to find. It does not take a genius to predict that today's modern cars will be a nightmare to maintain and repair five to ten years from now. If you plan to buy a used car, pay great attention to the reliability of the car's computer systems and related technology. Test reports on the internet may help you make good decisions.
- Having different technology platforms and incompatible devices in the same household: Maintaining different technology platforms (e.g., laptops, smartphones) can lead to additional costs and time spent maintaining these platforms, fixing malfunctions, or buying spare parts (e.g., replacing a forgotten charger when on vacation). Therefore, my wife and I always use the same type of laptop and phone models. This way we know how to fix issues

ourselves and can help each other out (e.g., use each other's charger and cables or those from previously owned models).

Not all examples of excessive complexity have to do with technology. Unnecessary complexity can become an inflation trap in non-technology aspects of our lives as well:

- Being involved in an excessively high number of activities with different organizations (e.g., volunteer work, a parish, children's school groups, sports teams), leading to an organizational and logistical complexity nightmare.
- Having many items of clothing, but a lack of coordinated outfits. This often requires buying additional items when attending a formal function or business event.
- Lack of routines for recurring tasks (e.g., going shopping without having an organized list of items regularly bought).
- Lack of prioritization of activities leading to the feeling of being overwhelmed and lost.
- Procrastination leading to a time bottleneck in the future and overwhelming stress. Such stress then forces us to make quick decisions often leading to inefficient and more expensive solutions (e.g., procrastinating the booking of a vacation trip).
- Committing to an excessive number of unrelated and non-standard investments leading to time-consuming administrative efforts (e.g., oversight, administration, tax requirements, financial management).

There are many more examples of value-destroying complexity. Again, such complexity leads to higher costs, waste of valuable time, and, often, unproductive mental agitation.

#8: AVOID BOOMERANG COSTS

Boomerang costs are additional costs that emerge after an initial transaction or activity has been executed. The most striking example is the production of electricity through nuclear power plants. Electricity produced and consumed in one year creates additional future costs for storing nuclear waste. These future costs create a substantial inflation risk. For example, many countries pay large sums of money for storing nuclear waste that was used to generate electricity in the 1970s. Needless to say, these costs will continue for hundreds of years into the future. In other words, future generations will still pay for electricity we produced and used in the past.

There are many examples of boomerang costs. Buying a computer printer requires you to keep buying expensive print cartridges. The cost of print cartridges is typically a multiple of the amount paid for the printer. Few people choose the printer they buy by evaluating the boomerang cost of buying over-priced print cartridges. Many printers do not accept cheaper ink cartridges from third parties.

Boomerang costs are a huge inflation problem as the costs will occur in the future, exposing you to a big inflation risk. In fact, high inflation can turn boomerang costs into your biggest inflation nightmare.

Boomerang costs appear in all aspects of modern life. Your Beat Inflation strategy must identify your exposure to boomerang costs and initiate corrective action where needed. For example:

- Avoid buying cheap and low-quality products (e.g., water faucets, toilet bowls, bathroom fixtures, kitchen appliances), which are prone to become a boomerang cost problem. The initial savings are likely to be dwarfed by the future costs of rectifying problems. Repairs, damages due to malfunction (e.g., leaking pipes), or early replacement of faulty products create substantial boomerang costs. Choose quality solutions by checking product reviews on the internet and read consumer reports. When in doubt, choose higher quality.
- When you renovate your house or conduct maintenance repairs, choose respected companies that are known for high

quality work. This is particularly important for plumbing, electrical, and roofing work, which may create expensive boomerang costs if the initial work was of poor quality.

- Excessively complex systems or solutions will lead to high boomerang costs in the future. Strive for simplicity.
- Avoid the purchase of exotic, extra-ordinary, or rare products to prevent future expensive costs for spare parts and maintenance.
- When designing your garden, think of costs in terms of the future (e.g., bamboo plants might be nice to look at, but may create significant boomerang costs for future containment or removal).
- Poor lifestyle choices (e.g., poor nutrition, irregular sleeping habits, lack of exercise) are likely to create significant future health care expenses.
- Pets may expose you to future expensive boomerang costs, particularly if your pet is fed an unhealthy diet.
- Buying an oversized house can lead to higher costs (e.g., real estate taxes, repairs, maintenance, home owner association fees, insurance, mortgage payments). Unless you rent out parts of your house, these costs are not covered by any income generated from the house. Therefore, rightsizing is an important activity.
- Driving a foreign luxury car can create substantial costs as repairs, maintenance, and insurance are typically significantly higher than those for standard cars.

#9: COMPARE YOUR OWN SPENDING WITH THAT OF RELATIVES, FRIENDS, AND COLLEAGUES (BENCHMARKING)

Comparing your spending data with that of relatives, friends, or colleagues is a powerful activity. Management consultants call such an activity "competitive benchmarking." It is part of the standard consulting tool kit. Competitive benchmarking is not an intellectual challenge.

Everybody can do it and it can be done fast. After completing the task, the results become immediately obvious.

Now let us take this tool from the corporate world and use it for our purposes. We need to decompose our total cost block and allocate it to different activities (see Chart 27).

Next, ask members of your Beat Inflation team or friends and family to conduct the same activity. It is important that you use identical cost buckets. Otherwise, your results will be misleading. Once this is done, you can start comparing the different cost structures.

Whenever you find significant deviations, conduct further analysis. You want to find out why you pay more than others (or vice versa) and determine what action is needed to reverse this situation.

For example, many subscription services use automatic renewal to push through price increases. Your bill for this service will increase every year, often far above actual inflation rates. Sometimes, it just takes one phone call to achieve a significant price reduction.

However, to be the most effective, you need to know the market rate or best-practice examples. This is why you need the results of a benchmarking exercise. Knowing the actual costs for other people gives you the most powerful arguments to (re)negotiate the prices you will pay in the future. Significant cost reductions are possible, particularly if the economy starts to weaken due to inflation. Companies would rather reduce your price than lose you as a customer.

When consultants do this work with big corporations, they typically focus on bigger cost categories before they drill down to smaller ones as this is more efficient. However, since our personal finances are much less complicated, it may make sense to include all cost categories in our analysis.

CHART 27: Benchmarking Your Cost Structure (select examples)

Cost Item	My Cost	Best bench-mark	Next steps/timing	Status
Home repairs (specify)				
Home insurance				
Car insurance				
Health insurance				
Mobile phones				
Home internet				
Cable television				
Home phone				
Gym membership				
Water bill				
Electricity bill				
Gardener cost				
Streaming services				
Magazine subscriptions				

Feel free to add categories as appropriate.

Benchmarking the costs of each relevant line item will create countless ideas for cost-cutting activities. Now that you have created cost transparency, you can approach vendors to demand a deal at much improved rates. It is quite powerful to start your negotiation with "I know that others pay price X. I want to be treated equally."

When you fill out this chart, it is important to define concrete next steps with a completion date. Control your progress by filling out the Status column using completion percentages or colored circles (green if you are making progress or red if you are behind schedule). Find a way that works for you.

Inflation insight:

Comparing your cost data and structure with others is only the first step. It is useless if you do not approach vendors and stores and demand better deals.

In addition, it may be helpful to benchmark your spending by category. This is a little bit more work, but if you believe that you are not very effective or efficient in controlling your spending, this is a valuable activity.

Benchmarking data is extremely powerful and an essential requirement for saving money. It easily identifies areas in which you overspend (or underspend). For example, you may go overboard when it comes to eating in restaurants. In that case, the analysis in Chart 28 would show much higher spending levels for you compared to your peer group.

Chart 28: Benchmarking Your Costs by Category

Category	Your spending		Bench-mark		Next steps	Status
	In $	In %	In $	In %		
Housing						
Food						
Groceries						
Clothes						
Transportation						
Education						
Insurance						
Tech/Media[17]						
Entertainment						
Travel/vacation						
Other (define)						

Change the categories as your situation dictates. This is not an academic exercise. Using estimates is fine as long as these estimates are valid and honest. Your benchmark data may also be obtained from reputable websites on the internet, which may offer benchmark data on cost items. However, you may need to adjust such data for regional differences.

Once you have obtained all required data, you can look for cost-cutting opportunities, including rebalancing your spending habits.

---

[17] This category includes all phone-related, internet, cable TV, streaming services, and data storage expenses.

For example, if your spending in the tech/media category is triple the amount of what other people spend, you should immediately do some further analysis (e.g., compare each line item to identify concrete cost-cutting opportunities).

You may also use the data obtained by this analysis for future financial budgeting. Setting strict spending limits can help bring more discipline into your financial management.

#10: FIND HIGH IMPACT, BEST-PRACTICE EXAMPLES EMPLOYED BY OTHERS AND COPY THEM

According to an old saying, you can achieve anything in life, but nothing alone. The same is true for beating inflation. This is why I recommend building a Beat Inflation team. Beating inflation is much easier when you use the strength, experience, and wisdom of a team.

One way to find additional cost-cutting ideas is simply to talk to as many people as possible. Ask whether they have recently succeeded in reducing their expenses. The more people you talk to the more ideas will be generated.

There are many more approaches available to you to find best-practice examples:

- Pose questions on social media platforms. My experience is that people like to share their experiences and to help others. You may learn about new strategies to fight inflation that you have not yet contemplated.
- On social media platforms, look for groups that are focused on this topic and join those that are appropriate. Alternatively, you may consider creating your own group.
- Invite friends, colleagues, neighbors, or relatives who are not members of your Beat Inflation team to join you to brainstorm about cost-

cutting ideas. New perspectives are always helpful. Carefully observe what they are doing.

- Search the internet for best-practice examples. Read articles written by others on the subject of household cost management.
- Try to find people with practical inflation management experiences. For example, Venezuelans who have recently experienced hyperinflation have accumulated valuable experiences and lessons learned. Try to meet people from other countries and learn from their experience.

In conclusion, cost cutting is a critical activity to reduce your inflation gap. It may not be sufficient to completely close the gap on its own, but it is likely to contribute a substantial amount to your financial bottom line. Cost cutting has a decisive advantage over other measures as it has an immediate impact on your financial situation. Additionally, investing the cost savings create future investment income. You gain twice.

Therefore, you should start your cost-cutting activities right now. This chapter provided you with ten different sub-activities of the first core activity. There is no particular order to these sub-activities. Doing and implementing is more important than the actual sequence you choose.

And please do not forget: Analysis without enforcement is a waste of time. Do not stop after the analysis stage of your activities. Finish the task by implementing an idea or decision. This is the only way to reduce your expenses. And last, do not be shy to ask for a discount or any form of price reduction. Make it part of your DNA. You will be surprised how much money you can save with a simple question.

CHAPTER 7: DECREASE YOUR RISK (CORE ACTIVITY #2)

Introductory comments:

A successful balancing of opportunities and risks is a necessary condition for achieving a successful, fulfilled, and happy life. There is an impact asymmetry between opportunities and risks: You can miss hundreds of highly attractive opportunities in life and still become highly successful and wealthy. However, it may take just one severe risk event for which you failed to prepare adequately to wipe out your past success and, in extreme cases, your way of life. Therefore, risk management must always be on your radar screen.

Most people overly focus on opportunities and neglect the associated risks. This is a dangerous mistake. Keep both balanced, particularly during volatile and risky periods of excessive inflation.

In this chapter we will pursue the following two victories:

Victory 1 (short-term inflation focus): *In the short term, we need to closely monitor the risks we are exposed to. A period of high inflation is a high-risk period. We should cut our risk taking wherever possible and whenever a risk is not justified by an outsized opportunity. Our risk monitoring is not confined to financial risks. We need to take a broader perspective that includes health risks and location risk.*

Victory 2 (long-term personal growth): *To be successful over the long term, we need to have black belt expertise in balancing risks and opportunities. This requires us to understand how to assess risks and how to balance them with opportunities. We need to be patient. Occasionally, life rewards us with situations that promise outsized opportunities that come with limited risks. Such opportunities are the ones we want to* *pursue. Also, preparedness is an important concept in risk management. It can turn a severe risk into an attractive opportunity.*

It is important to pay close attention to your overall approach to risk taking during a period of high inflation, which can lead to severe disruptions, increased uncertainty, and inferior outlooks for economic and political developments. More specifically, past periods of high inflation or even hyperinflation were accompanied by major negative disruptions (risks) such as:

- Severe recessions
- Turbulent financial markets
- Political and social disorder
- Dramatic rises of unemployment
- Spread of poverty and food insecurity

Therefore, a cautious and reflective approach to risk taking may be advantageous for those with a low-risk appetite, insufficient risk management skills, and limited risk absorption capacity.

> During my management consulting career, I have spent a lot of time on risk management projects. One of the most important lessons I learned is that the borders between risks and opportunities are fluent. More specifically, the same disruptive event can be a risk to some people and an opportunity for others. For example, the arrival and spread of the internet put many companies out of business. However, for others the internet was a gold mine with endless opportunities. I encourage you whenever you encounter a risk in life, seek for ways to turn it into an opportunity. This is what highly successful people try to do. Often, diligent preparedness strategies can transform a severe risk into an attractive opportunity.

SOME MOTIVATING THOUGHTS ABOUT THE POWER OF RISK MANAGEMENT

For many of you, thinking about risks in general, and your personal risks in particular, is uncomfortable. This is even more true during disruptive periods. However, the discipline of risk management is not meant to scare you but to help you develop strategies that limit, lower, or even eliminate your risk exposure. It should help you sleep well at night and not toss and turn.

Risk management mistakes are not easily forgiven. They can get punished brutally. Therefore, our focus should be to build a defensive wall around us for protection. This wall consists of one major building material: preparedness.

For me, preparedness is one of the most important key factors of success in life. It works well at any time period, not only during times of crises. Employed correctly, the wall we create will give us peace of mind and safety.

Obviously, employing preparedness strategies has one drawback: We will prepare for a high number of risk events that will never materialize. However, it is comforting to know that no matter what happens, you will be prepared. You won't cancel your car insurance just because you did not have a car accident last year. The goal is to neutralize risks that we are not willing to take.

Preparedness is not a new strategy. It was often employed by our parents and grandparents during times of uncertainty. You can trace back the concept of preparedness over thousands of years.

As a middle and high school student in Trier, Germany, my walk to school let me pass the cathedral of Trier, a building whose history can be traced back to Roman times. On one tower of the cathedral is a clock with the inscription: *Nescitis dominus venit.* It refers to the gospel of Matthew

(24:42), which reminds passerby to be prepared at all times as we do not know the exact hour when the Lord will arrive. I found this an incredible inspiration for practicing preparedness in my life. Today, it might mean that you cannot precisely time the arrival of a severe risk event. Hence, let us be prepared at any time.

One last thought. Some of you may still feel the pain of recent inflation management mistakes (e.g., investments that turned negative due to the recent inflation shock). If this happens, do not be too harsh with yourself. Past decisions are a matter for your mistake book: document them, learn from them, and never repeat them. That is all you can do; move on and don't get stuck in the past. A much better future is not only possible, but also likely to happen if you learn from past mistakes and prepare for future opportunities.

During the 1970s inflation crisis, the most astute and respected CEOs made countless mistakes. Thus, you are not alone. It is now important to look forward and increase your defensive capabilities and preparedness. Let the past be the past.

Let us start with the most important risk management activity: assessing your overall inflation vulnerability and identifying issues that require corrective action.

VULNERABILITY ASSESSMENT

It is important to understand your own personal vulnerability to high inflation. This is a demanding task, because everybody's situation is different. There isn't any simple five-minute test that tells you your vulnerability. However, the thoughts presented in this chapter may give you a head start in understanding your personal vulnerability to inflation.

This vulnerability assessment is meant to be general in nature, as every person faces a different situational context. You need to tailorize this framework to your specific situation. The following additional activities may help you with this task:

- Deepen your analysis and add questions that are specific to your situation (e.g., special circumstances, known future life events, professional and career issues).
- Contact members of your Beat Inflation team to validate your assessments. Let other members of the team do an "outside-in" assessment of your vulnerability. This may add new perspectives and new insights.
- Ask people you know with inflation experience to weigh in as well. For example, you may have friends or colleagues in other countries who experienced painful periods of inflation and may offer valuable insights.

To get started with your vulnerability assessment, you may wish to consider the following twelve questions:

12 VULNERABILITY QUESTIONS

1. Assume your living expenses double over the next seven years. Are you confident that you can handle this cost explosion? How? Through salary increases?
2. Are you mission critical for your employer in that you are recognized as someone who creates great value and is hard to replace? Is your employer afraid of losing you? Only mission-critical employees have the bargaining power to ask for salary increases that offset actual inflation. Why are you mission critical? What skills and capabilities make you unique?
3. Assume your employer is forced to close down. Do you have a standing job offer from another company or could you line up an equally attractive job within a week? If yes, who would hire you? Why? When was the last time you spoke with this potential employer? Would they hire you even if the economy deteriorates into a severe recession?
4. Do you (or your partner) have marketable skills that could be used for generating extra income to close the inflation gap? What are these skills/capabilities and how much extra money could you make with a side activity?
5. Do you have enough savings to cover an unexpected hit to your income (e.g., no bonus payment, losing your job) or a major unexpected expense?
6. Could you cover your expenses for one year without being employed? How many months/years could you survive financially without being employed?
7. Does your health enable you to perform well at your current job and to work extra hours to generate additional income if needed? Is your good health protecting you from rising health care costs?
8. Are you regionally or– (even better) internationally mobile to exploit better job or living opportunities if your current location is exceptionally hard hit by inflation and its likely consequences (e.g., job loss, crime, deteriorating living conditions)? Do you fulfill basic

requirements for a regional/international move (e.g., work permits, visa, professional certifications, relevant business contacts/network, language skills, experience, and mindset)?

9. Do you have additional skills that allow you to work in a different field/industry should your current career make you unemployable? Do you have relevant experiences in alternative careers?
10. Do you have a strong network of business contacts, friends, acquaintances, active membership in trade associations, or family relationships that could help you find a new job quickly during disruptive periods?
11. Are you exposed to financial inflation risks such as variable rate debt, excessive debt (that needs to be refinanced soon), or unaddressed future (re-)financing needs?
12. Are your investments well diversified and resilient to inflation shocks? Do you use a professional financial advisor with a solid knowledge of inflation management? Do you actively ask for a second opinion on important financial matters?

Do not be shocked if you answered "no" several times. This test is to identify your inflation vulnerability. The next step is to address these issues. Understanding your vulnerability is key for crafting a sound Beat Inflation strategy. Many of the ideas that might help you address your inflation vulnerabilities will be discussed in different chapters of this book. The goal is to develop a personal strategy that will significantly improve your inflation readiness.

THE GOAL OF RISK MANAGEMENT

Most people still do not understand the essence of sophisticated risk management. Risk management is not about blindly eliminating all risks in your life. Doing so would create a miserable life and, more importantly, a riskier one as well. Without risk taking your success in life is capped at a low level.

Any activity in life exposes you to risks, but it also exposes you to opportunities. Switching employers to get a promotion and a higher salary is a risk. However, it is one worth taking if you did a decent due diligence on your new employer.

Risk management involves balancing the opportunities we pursue with their associated risks. You cannot separate the two.

> REMINDER: RISK MANAGEMENT IN LIFE:
>
> Risk management seeks to balance the opportunities we pursue with their associated short and long-term risks. You cannot separate opportunities from their associated risks.

Once you identify risk imbalances or vulnerabilities, you can choose one or more of the following risk management strategies to mitigate the risk:

- **Risk elimination:** This is the simplest action step. If an activity is associated with an excessive risk, you simply stop the activity.
- **Risk reduction:** In this case, you continue with the activity but you engage in action steps to reduce your risk exposure (e.g., wear protective gear when performing a dangerous activity).
- **Risk hedging:** You transfer (part) of the risk to someone else (e.g., you buy an insurance policy).
- **Risk diversification:** You lower your overall risk exposure by avoiding concentrated risk situations (e.g., diversify your investments across different asset classes and/or geographies).

FIVE INFLATION-SPECIFIC RISK BUCKETS THAT MAY NEED CORRECTIVE ACTION

Everybody's risk situation is different. However, there are five common risk categories that may require specific attention during periods of high inflation (Chart 29):

CHART 29: Five Specific Focus Points for Inflation Risk Management

1 Secure your primary job

- Secure your current job
- Have an alternative lined up (just in case)

2 Decision making risks

- Inflation is unforgiving, mistakes will be punished
- Making superb decisions is a key necessity for beating inflation

3 Health risks

- Health care cost inflation on its own can destabilize your financial stability
- Good health helps dealing with the extra work and mental stress caused by high inflation

4 Financial risks

- How can I improve my financial risk exposure?

5 Location and mobility risk

- How protected is my current location from inflation risks?
- Am I ready to relocate if high inflation makes my current location unlivable

The first risk category will be discussed in the following chapter. Let us focus on the remaining four:

Decision-making risks

The quality of your decisions will greatly determine how well you get through the inflation period. There is very little tolerance for mistakes, unfortunately. Therefore, it is important to focus on your decision-making processes and employ critical thinking wherever appropriate. Also, do not let anybody pressure you into making fast decisions. Make important decisions only if you have taken the time to do a proper analysis.

Personal Observation:

I have just completed a book *entitled Superperformers – Why Winners Win and Losers Lose*.[18] I compare the strategies and habits employed by highly successful people with those used by average performers. One key finding was that Superperformers are relatively slow when making consequential decisions. In fact, their zest for reducing uncertainty often leads to additional analysis and research. This "slowness" is sometimes hard to understand for less successful people, who wrongly believe that fast decision making is always a good thing. It is not, particularly not during disruptive periods.

The impressive success of those who are Superperformers clearly proves: slowness often beats speed in life.

It is important to differentiate between consequential and inconsequential decisions. The latter you can do with speed and less analysis, the former you cannot.

When making consequential decisions do not rush. Seek to understand the details or ask a friend with expertise to support you. Always have rigorous analysis precede your decision making, as conceptualized in the Critical Thinking Success Chain (Chart 30).

[18] To be published in early 2023.

Chart 30: The Critical Thinking Success Chain[19]

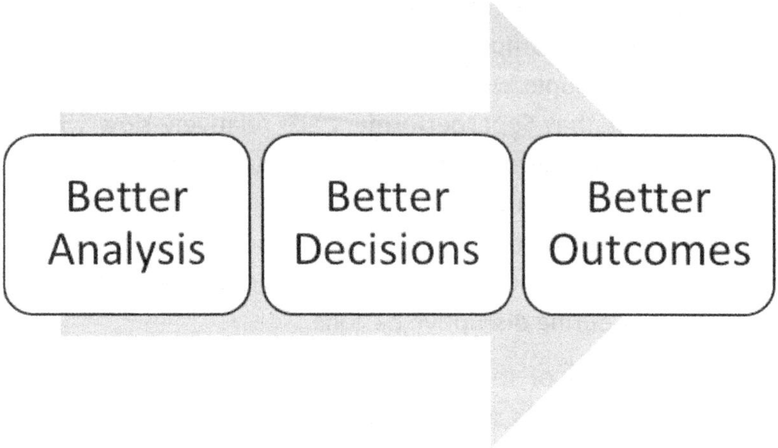

Understand that there are two worlds out there (see Chart 31): The first one is the "I Guess" world, in which decisions are made based on guesses and assumptions. This is where unsuccessful people live and where risks are high. The second world is the one where successful people live. It is called the "I Know" world, in which important decisions are made based on rigorous analysis. Risks are low in the latter. You choose in which world you want to live.

[19] Hammes: Success through Critical Thinking, (2019), page 18.

Chart 31: Decision Making in an *I Guess World* Versus an *I Know World*[20]

I Guess World	***I Know World***
• Linear extrapolation of past trends • Follow conventional wisdom and established practices • Follow others without due diligence checks • Superficial analysis that lacks depth, scope, completeness, or time horizon • Use of unverified data • Unwilling to change or revise decisions, even if new data or reasoning raise doubts about conclusions • Unwilling to test hypotheses and beliefs	• Attitude of constructive skepticism when it comes to trends, assumptions, established practices, and decision making • Personally conduct in-depth, fact-based, complete analysis • Verification of data sources • Never rush into important decisions • Open to change/revise decisions when new facts become available • Willing to question and challenge own hypotheses and beliefs

Improving the quality of all consequential decisions should become a key focus that will help us close the inflation gap.

Health risks

There are two crucial reasons why you should focus on your health, particularly during periods of high inflation.

First, health care costs have a tendency to increase even faster than reported inflation rates. In other words, poor health can become a big financial problem. Therefore, neglecting your health is a major financial risk (apart from the fact that it significantly lowers your quality of life).

[20] Hammes: Success through Critical Thinking (2019), page 34.

Keep in mind that periods of high inflation can last for a decade or longer. Poor health and lifestyle choices made today may financially disadvantage you in the future. In other words, poor health not only ruins your daily life, it is also a financial liability.

Second, implementing the many activities required by the DVBI program requires some extra energy. Being in good health can provide you with the energy level needed to perform with maximum concentration and commitment. This is particularly important when you seek salary increases and promotions at work.

The challenges posed by high inflation should be a great motivator to get you more focused on healthy lifestyle issues. Luckily, there is a lot of information available for those interested in this topic as well as qualified health care professionals who are eager to help.

It also may make sense to invest some time into health education. Many people have serious gaps in their understanding of simple human biology, nutrition, and healthy lifestyle choices. Now is the time to close this gap.

Last, engaging in excessively dangerous activities (certain sports with high injury risk) without proper risk management practices (e.g., wearing protective equipment) is also worth reflecting on. As losing your job is your biggest inflation risk, dangerous leisure activities should be part of your inflation vulnerability assessment. This is particularly important if such activities are not covered by insurance or if you may lose your job due to injury.

Financial risks

During times of economic crisis, financial risk management becomes of highest importance. Inflation is unforgiving. It rarely offers you a second chance for rectifying past mistakes. Therefore, you should assign financial risk management a high priority within your DVBI program.

In general, during times of disruption and economic crisis, two ideas come to mind: risk reduction and risk diversification.

- **Risk reduction:** I have a simple rule for myself: When in doubt, do not take a risk. This is a simple, although quite powerful, rule. Risks that you are not fully comfortable with are in most cases not worth taking. Either you raise your comfort level by collecting additional information and conducting more research, or you simply walk away from a risky situation.
- **The importance of diversification:** No one can exactly predict how inflation will impact a country's economy and financial markets. Those outcomes are the result of collective decision making and, in some cases, accidental developments.
  Consequently, taking concentrated risk (e.g., a huge investment in one stock) is a very dangerous strategy. Do you have the risk absorption capacity to deal with a significant loss if things work out differently than expected? Diversification of your risk exposure is a good way to deal with an uncertain environment. Don't put all your eggs in one basket.

The key to good financial risk management is anticipation, caution, and taking early corrective action if circumstances require doing so. Do not wait until your financial situation creates a major challenge. It is important to seek the help of qualified professionals to support you with this challenging task.

Location and mobility risks

In some cases, inflation may spiral out of control and make your current location an unattractive place to live. In such situations, a move to another, cheaper region within your country or to a different country may be required. While such moves may present social setbacks (at least temporarily), they are sometimes the only path to escape inflation pressure.

During the inflation crisis in Venezuela, we witnessed millions of people seeking to leave the country. Those who had the required documentation (e.g., visa, foreign and domestic passport), language skills, education, and connections were quick to make the move. In most cases, such international moves worked well when compared to the situation at home.

Unfortunately, the exodus of highly qualified people made the situation worse for those who stayed. The brain-drain in many Venezuelan industries reliant on highly skilled workers led to further deterioration.

The lesson learned is that having mobility options in place is a valuable strategy. You hope that you will not need to exploit such options. However, once you do need them it is too late to prepare.

I hope that at the end of this chapter you now understand the importance of anticipatory risk management. Again, the goal is to identify future inflation risks before they materialize and use the time to prepare for them. In many cases, you can mitigate these risks if you start early. In some cases, you may even be able to turn inflation risks into opportunities. That would be a splendid outcome. The next chapter talks more about this important topic of capturing opportunities.

CHAPTER 8: INCREASE YOUR INCOME (CORE ACTIVITY #3)

Introductory comments:

For many readers, this will be the most exciting chapter of this book. Understandably, earning more is a shared goal for all employees, business owners, and entrepreneurs. Without any doubt, it is a goal that is achievable for everybody. However, we need a strategic and coordinated approach to exploit the opportunities available to us. Achieving the following two victories can radically improve your life. Use this opportunity!

In this chapter we will pursue the following two victories:

Victory 1 (short-term inflation focus): *We need to first secure our current job and increase our bargaining power to demand salary increases that ideally offset inflation. We accomplish this by not simply counting the hours until we can go home, but by approaching our job as a professional. Taking pride in what we are doing and delivering the best we can do every day will enable us to demand a higher salary.*

Victory 2 (long-term personal growth): *Once we approach our current job with pride and a professional attitude, we signal to our employers and to others (e.g., competitors, customers, vendors) that we are ready to step up and assume more responsibilities (i.e., get a promotion). In addition, we will develop our entrepreneurial mindset to capture additional opportunities that are plentiful in today's modern economy (e.g., generate passive income).*

Your income from your job is an important pillar of your Beat Inflation strategy. One of the biggest risks you face is losing your job during a period of high inflation as this will immediately increase your inflation gap. Unfortunately, periods of high inflation often coincide with economic weakness and rising unemployment.

Therefore, it is crucial to do everything in your power to secure your current job. Ideally, you already have alternative job offers lined up in case your employer is forced to cut its workforce or to shut down its operations. Because the latter can happen during periods of high inflation, you need to be prepared.

It is important to understand that every job is full of hidden opportunities. Unfortunately, few people understand this important topic. The minute you show up at work, you are in the spotlight of customers, vendors, colleagues, supervisors, and many others. Remember that many of the people you interact with could hold the key to much better job opportunities (e.g., promotions, job offers from other companies). You will only receive this key to a better and more successful life if you consistently impress others.

Unfortunately, the latter is the problem. Many people perform their job with little passion and excitement. They do only what is required to not get in trouble. If those people interact with a customer who may be looking to fill a higher paid job in their company, they will not land on the list of possible candidates.

I once read of a sales person working in the fresh produce department of a German grocery store. He approached his job with excitement every day. One day, a customer showed up with her husband, who was looking to hire highly motivated sales people for a new financial product. The husband was so impressed by the worker's sales skills and positive attitude that he extended an offer to the store employee, who had never worked in a financial institution. The husband knew it was easier to teach a person basic finance skills than to find someone with an exciting attitude and great sales skills.

Lesson learned: Show your best self every day at work. You never know who may be watching.

Therefore, securing your current job is initially more important than thinking about expanding your income base. The good news is that the two activities are closely linked. The activities securing your current job will also make you eligible for a salary increase.

In a nutshell, your goal is to become mission critical to your employer. If you are hard to replace, your employer may be more willing to raise your salary.

In this chapter, we address the following three sub-activities:

1. Secure your current job
2. Achieve salary increases that, ideally, offset inflation rates
3. Develop an entrepreneurial mindset and generate additional income

SUB-ACTIVITY 1: SECURE YOUR CURRENT JOB

There are five key activities that help you increase your job security (and receive a salary increase in the future).

1. **First- class attitude:** One of the key parameters in evaluating an employee's performance is attitude. People with a poor attitude toward work are typically the first ones to be let go in an economic downturn. This is a pity, because it is so easy to improve our attitude. Also, a good attitude makes the time spent at work

easier and more fulfilling. We will enjoy our work environment if we maintain our best attitude. Keep in mind, the assessment of your attitude is a subjective activity. Your supervisor's perception of your attitude and your own perception may be quite different. Therefore, it is important that you judge your attitude from your supervisor's perspective. Ask yourself: How happy are they with my performance? Do they trust me with more difficult or more important tasks?

In addition, you need to keep in mind that your co-workers' perceptions are important as well. Whatever co-workers tell your supervisor about you will impact their perception of you. Therefore, do not only perform well when your supervisor is around. Make it a habit to show up with a first-class attitude all the time.

Here is a list of ideas that may help you accomplish this goal:

- Always arrive ahead of time at work. Never leave exactly on time. Stay a few minutes extra to finish what you were doing. Do not show up late at a client meeting, internal meeting, or a conference call.
- No matter what activity you are asked to perform, do it with enthusiasm, pride, and joy.
- Be grateful for having your current job, do not take it for granted.
- Do not engage in spreading gossip.
- Get a reputation for being more of a problem solver and less of a problem finder.
- Always help others if they need a hand; be known as an empathic and supportive person.
- Always be emotionally controlled if you discuss controversial issues or have a different opinion. Never become personal in an argument; never engage in shouting matches or show emotional

outbursts. Discuss issues in a constructive and open-minded manner.

- Be focused at work. Don't get caught looking at your smartphone all the time or succumb to other distractions. Work time is for work.

2. **Show that you care about the company and its success:**

- Always show an interest in the well-being of the company. Ask your supervisor how sales are doing in your part of the organization. Offer your help for any project that could help improve sales or win new customers.
- Read newspaper articles about your industry, your company, and competitors. Stay informed about industry trends.
- Defend your company's reputation in public. Be a great ambassador for your company.

3. **Take initiative and present solutions:** Employers love employees who take initiative. Here are some ideas how you can do so at your current job:

- If you encounter a problem at work, always think about a possible solution when reporting the problem to your supervisor. This way you will be seen as a problem solver and not as someone who constantly finds fault.
- Take initiative to fix smaller issues if possible. For example, cleaning up a small spill is more impressive than waiting for the office cleaning staff to do so.
- Try to be proactive and solve problems before your supervisor notices them (but make sure you get the credit).
- Impress clients and vendors with your proactiveness and attitude. You want them to tell your supervisor how well you performed.

4. **Ask for feedback**: Asking for detailed feedback is the best way to demonstrate that you take your job seriously and that you care about your standing in the company. Here are some ideas on this topic:

- Ask for feedback on your work outside of scheduled performance reviews. It shows high engagement. Also, it helps to understand issues early and to address them before they are written up in a formal performance review.
- Do not be defensive when you are criticized. Do not get emotional or personal. You can state that you are surprised about negative feedback or criticism, but such replies need to come with a positive statement promising to do better in the future.
- If you believe that criticism was not justified, make an effort to address the issue and to "over-deliver" on your work performance going forward (i.e., "show them, don't tell them"). In a few weeks, ask your supervisor whether you improved and performed to their standard.

5. **Learn new skills:**

- Ask your supervisor for guidance on what additional skills you should acquire. Then put these suggestions into action.
- Get a reputation for being someone always working on expanding their skill portfolio.
- Turn your knowledge and learning into a reputation of being the go-to person for difficult problems.

Some readers may believe that these suggestions are not important or are too much work. Let me assure you, as somebody who has managed large groups of people, they are important and they count when making decisions on salary increases, promotions, or headcount reductions.

What I have described is the ideal employee from a supervisor's perspective. You want to come as close as possible. After a few weeks of delivering your best self at work, you are likely to enjoy work much more than in the past. Your co-workers will approach you in a different way and you will feel a sense of pride and accomplishment. Over time, your "new self" will become your "normal self" and you will be unable to imagine the way you approached work in the past.

Unfortunately, because many employees fail at this simple task, they miss out on future opportunities.

SUB-ACTIVITY 2: ACHIEVE SALARY INCREASES THAT, IDEALLY, OFFSET INFLATION RATES

The period of German hyperinflation (1921–1923) had a disastrous impact on most middle- and lower-class families. Many families ended up in severe poverty, including highly educated individuals with respected careers.

For example, university professors, high school teachers, museum directors, and senior public servants were trapped by high inflation. The issue was that their employers did not raise their salaries sufficiently. While they remained employed, the salary they received lagged significantly behind actual inflation rates. This was a recipe for the steady erosion of living standards and wealth destruction.

The key issue these people faced was a lack of employee bargaining power vis-à-vis their current employers. Bargaining power means that you are in some way mission critical to your employer. If your employer is afraid to lose you to a higher paying competitor, they may be willing to raise your salary and issue bonus payments.

Bargaining power comes from a variety of sources. In general, it correlates with the importance of your job to the overall success of the company and the difficulty of replacing you with someone equally qualified at lower cost. A plumber with special training, experience, and skills is mission critical to a plumbing company and can demand salary increases that match or even exceed inflation rates. On the other hand, an administrative aide in the same company can usually be replaced easily at lower cost. Highly trained engineers in charge of critical infrastructure maintenance have bargaining power; employees of cultural institutions (e.g., museums) unfortunately do not. Although the latter may not lose their jobs due to inflation, they lack the bargaining power to demand inflation-beating salary increases.

There is a lot you can do to increase your bargaining power in your company prior to or during the outbreak of an inflation crisis. Most employees neglect the important function of weatherproofing their careers against inflation. They simply believe that the good times will continue. By failing to increase their competitive advantage in the job market, they face an even higher inflation risk. You and your dependents will pay a hefty price if you fail to build enough bargaining power in the job market.

In other words, your problem is not only keeping your job. You must also ensure that your job compensates you for lost purchasing power due to inflation. Doing so is essential for closing the inflation gap. The answer is: make yourself irreplaceable and be prepared to always have a new job lined up in case you lose your current one. This is one of the most effective inflation protection strategies you can choose.

A commitment to lifelong learning and skill building:

We are living in a world where access to education has never been easier and cheaper. Education in its pure form, defined as the acquisition of knowledge, has become practically free for many relevant skills.[21] Many highly ranked universities put their classes on the internet for free. Professors from reputable schools teach classes on learning platforms that cost a fraction of what is charged at a university. Craftsmen of all kinds offer to teach relevant DIY skills, often on a professional level. You can learn many foreign languages through smart phone apps or internet platforms. In addition, many companies offer great training programs for their employees. It is up to you to use these opportunities.

The best protection against financial difficulties is to build your skill portfolio so that you always have the option to find a highly paid job, even during retirement. Lifelong learning is the strategy that will provide you with this valuable option. And it is fun as well.

Here are some ideas to increase your bargaining power in the job market:

- Acquire additional skills that are or will be relevant for your current or future employer, such as foreign language or computer/programming skills.
- Volunteer to accept mission-critical responsibilities.
- Acquire additional certifications that differentiate you from other employees and make you a scarce resource (e.g., obtain work-related certifications, become a notary, train as a first responder).

[21] Please note the difference between education and obtaining a degree from a reputable university, which is expensive in countries like the U.S. However, many countries offer free university education (e.g., Germany) and extend this option to academically qualified foreigners.

- Extend and deepen relationships with other people in your and other organizations (e.g., get to know people in other departments, build close relationships with customers, vendors, service providers).
- Take the lead for new initiatives such as organizing the company's social media presence or marketing its environmental impact track record.
- Become a role model within your company for exemplary behavior (e.g., discipline, self-organization, promoting team spirit).

If such strategies do not apply to your case, you may try a more conventional approach by focusing on the social role you play within your company. Fulfilling an important social role in an organization means that you create significant value to your employer by being a motivator, a "social historian" with documented knowledge and wisdom, a recognized conflict mediator, or a reliable event manager. You may be seen as the glue that holds the organization together. Top management often pays significant attention to employees playing such important social roles and views them as valuable social capital. In crises, such social capital is often what saves a company from degrading into panic and chaos.

During the financial crisis of 2007-2008, people with long experience in an industry or at their company (meaning they experienced past crises) who possessed social competence took a front seat in management discussions. It was not that they had technical knowledge other employees did not have. They had experienced past industry crises and became motivators when the office mood deteriorated. Some possessed special social skills that helped motivate and lead younger or less experienced colleagues. In fact, younger colleagues reached out to these more experienced people for guidance, comfort, and direction.

It does not hurt to have a contingency plan in place. High inflation typically comes with abnormally high unemployment rates. Therefore, you can never rely on being secure from getting fired, regardless of your performance. Your employer might go bankrupt due to a severe recession or being taken over by a competitor. Therefore, you need a "Monday morning plan" in case you lose your job on Friday. Here are some ideas for your contingency plan:

- Build a good relationship with suppliers, vendors, and service providers of your company. Build personal relationships with your counterparts; show an interest in their business and industry and try to expand your network into their organization. The more people you know outside of your own organization, the higher the chance to be on the radar screen for a new position outside your current employment.
- Get to know employees working at competitor organizations. Going to trade shows or conferences is an unsuspicious way to build new relationships and to deepen existing ones.
- Use social clubs, parishes, or charity events to network and to widen your circle of friends. Get to know as many people in different settings as possible.
- Connect to relevant people on social media networks. Tell them that you are interested in their industry and that you want to build new connections to people working in this field.
- Publish insightful posts on your industry or economic topics on social media. This is a great way to get noticed. You can do so by sharing newspaper articles with an inspiring comment attached.
- Comment on posts from people on social media. Try build a relationship with those who share your interests.

In conclusion, increasing your bargaining power through conduct, competence, responsibilities, or relationships is very important during periods of high inflation. Building strong relationships outside of your current employment raises your chances of being considered for new job opportunities. Do not focus your activities solely on your current employer. Include the outside world as much as possible.

SUB-ACTIVITY 3: DEVELOP AN ENTREPRENEURIAL MINDSET AND GENERATE ADDITIONAL INCOME

There is a fundamental difference between the 1970s inflation crisis and the one today. And this difference makes me optimistic for the future in general and for readers of this book in particular.

During the 1970s, high inflation met with a rigid, highly regulated, and inflexible labor market. In addition, there was no internet and no social media available for those looking for employment or networking opportunities. Education opportunities were scarce and expensive. Obviously, online courses did not exist. If you lost your job, you relied on newspaper ads or government offices to find a new one.

Even more importantly, the modern gig economy did not exist. The gig economy has democratized the option to become an entrepreneur, or at least a part-time entrepreneur (i.e., work at your job by day and sell your expertise at night). Some people use the gig economy to test the waters as an entrepreneur without taking the risk of leaving their current job until the time is right.

Modern technology has revolutionized the way we work and generate income. In general, there are five distinct differences between the 1970s inflation period and the one today:

- Transparency: You can find available jobs from home using your smart phone. This includes "mini-jobs," part-time employment, and full-time jobs.

- Self-promotion: You can advertise yourself and the skills you have on a global basis via webpage, video, blog, and so on.
- Remote work: Thanks to technology, we do not need to be physically present in an office. We can work remotely and globally regardless of our current residence. For example, an editor in the United States can work for a company in the United Kingdom.
- Gig economy: There is a global market for offering and searching for special skills in an informal setting. This has created a second job market that is growing rapidly and highly attractive.
- New entrepreneurial income opportunities: Attractive income opportunities have been created through modern technology. For example, the market for online courses has grown to over $300 billion US in 2021 and is expected to double over the next five years.[22] These courses provide training for a wide range of skills (e.g., playing a musical instrument, computer programming, gardening). As these courses are offered on a global scale, income opportunities are tremendous.

Technological progress is a source of great optimism for those willing to use it to their advantage and find new income opportunities. Not surprisingly, some people will find new careers or become full-time entrepreneurs. We are witnessing a revolution in the labor markets that is creating opportunities unheard of a decade ago.

Depending on your skill portfolio and interest, side jobs can be found in many different market places. Here are a few ideas (in addition to the obvious ones like working a shift in a retail store, restaurant, or grocery store):

- Working extra hours leveraging your skills, experience, and interest (e.g., plumbing, gardening, handyman work, painting).

[22] Based on average estimates found through internet research.

- Tutoring/teaching students. This can be particularly lucrative in the disciplines of mathematics, science, writing, and foreign languages.
- Buying, fixing, and selling used products in demand (e.g., bicycles, appliances, furniture, computer equipment).
- Creating or installing home decorations (e.g., blinds, window screens, shades). For example, ready-made window screens are often overpriced. Making them from scratch and selling them to interested customers is an easy job and may generate an attractive and permanent income source.
- Providing transportation (e.g., rides to an airport) are also easy ways to generate extra income.
- Joining an expert network: There are many social media-based networks that bring together experts (e.g., in business, finance, crafts, home repair) with those needing expertise. Depending on your level of expertise, you can generate attractive income by teaching your skills to companies and people in need of your expertise.

AN ATTRACTIVE STRATEGY: CREATING PASSIVE INFLATION-PROTECTED INCOME

Passive income is a relatively new field of generating attractive income streams. Keep in mind that the playground for generating passive income is practically unlimited. The ideas discussed in this section are only a small selection of what is available to you. Use these ideas to kick-start your search for and exploration of new opportunities. Do not let these ideas limit your creativity. Build on them, as the following example shows.

FROM POOL CLEANER TO ENTREPRENEUR: AN IMPRESSIVE TRANSFORMATION[23]

With the purchase of my first home in Florida, I also became the owner of my first swimming pool. I made the courageous decision to manage and maintain my pool myself, even though I had no prior experience. I luckily came across an expert pool cleaner on YouTube. His videos were excellent and saved me several times when tackling pool maintenance problems.

Recently, I looked him up again on the internet for a special pool maintenance problem. Over the years, this knowledgeable pool cleaner became quite an entrepreneur. His activity portfolio includes:

- a large collection of YouTube videos with more than 60 million views
- a merchandise business, where you can buy specialist products
- a coaching business for other pool cleaners
- a popular podcast
- sponsorships by many companies
- published books on pool cleaning

This person managed to turn his qualification and competence into an impressive collection of active and passive income businesses. He became a real entrepreneur.

Consider an apple tree. Once you have planted an apple tree, it takes about three to six years for the tree to bear fruit. Thereafter, the tree may produce fruit for about fifty years. A mature apple tree requires very little time from the owner. It just continues to produce apples year after year with minimal effort. You can then sell these apples at a farmer's market

[23] Please note that this case study is based on an outside-in analysis. No interviews were conducted. It is meant to encourage readers to explore their own opportunities for becoming passive/active income entrepreneurs.

or let people pick them themselves (you charge by the pound). Obviously, apple prices will go up with inflation. You are protected from inflation.

Understand the underlying principle of passive income opportunities: An initial money and/or time investment generates a future income stream with little or no additional time and effort required (like an apple tree).

Chart 32 describes the principles of passive income opportunity in more detail.

Chart 32: Passive Income Businesses to Beat Inflation

Characteristics of inflation-beating passive income activities
• Initial investment required (time and/or money) • Little or no investments needed after initial set-up • Creates annual income for an extended period of time • Future income rises with inflation • Limited risk for passive income initiator

There are countless opportunities available that fulfill the criteria for a passive income project. Here is a selection to kick-start your thinking. Use your creativity to create a passive income project that suits your situation.

WRITING A BOOK

Book publishing has changed dramatically over the past decades. Twenty years ago, an author needed an agent and a publisher to get a book to the market. Royalty from subsequent book sales were paltry. Most of the money went to the publisher and not to the author. For most people, book publishing was a not-for-profit activity.

This has changed dramatically with the advent of self-publishing. Today, anybody can publish a book at a fraction of the traditional costs. Activities formerly provided by publishing houses can now be bought from free-lancers around the world (e.g., the gig economy). This includes cover design, editing, proof-reading, and marketing. Even ghost writing is available through the internet.

Electronic platforms and print-on-demand technologies allow you to sell your books globally. Social media platforms allow you to promote your books for free.

Books can be sold in different delivery formats including hard cover, paperback, e-books, and audio books. Modern technology also allows you to lend your book against a fee. You can even sign up for a service that allows you to sell partial reading of your book.[24]

Please note that you can also sell your essays, documents, or presentations on internet platforms. It does not have to be a multi-page book.

Books fulfill all requirements of an inflation-beating passive income activity. After an initial limited investment, the author can enjoy a multi-year, inflation-protected cash-flow (assuming the book attracts readers).

Even better, the content created by the author can be monetized in many additional forms, including online tutorials, consulting activities, keynote speeches, workshops with companies, and videos on social media. In many cases, the author earns more from ancillary services than from the original book.

---

[24] For example, Amazon offers this service. The author receives a fee for the number of pages read online.

ONLINE CLASSES

The market for paid online classes has grown dramatically over the past decade. Future growth is expected to accelerate. Specialized platforms are available that support production, marketing, and global delivery. Everybody can create and sell an online course. All you need is a smartphone.

Online classes cover a wide spectrum of content. They range from cooking, learning to play a musical instrument, DIY activities, financial management, and academic instruction. Literally, any skill or competence can be sold as an online class. This option is particularly interesting for those who have published a book and seek to sell the content to a wider audience.

Very few technical investments are needed. Most platforms accept classes that are filmed with a regular smart phone. Editing software for video production often comes with your device. More professional video editing software is generally available for a small fee.

ROYALTY INCOME

Royalties are payments received for allowing a third party to use your (intellectual) property. Property in this context refers to a broad range of assets including musical compositions, movies, any form of copyrighted material, and software.

Three strategies are possible. First, you are the original owner of the intellectual property and you market it on your own. Second, you sell or license your intellectual property rights to a third party for them to market. Third, you are a marketing expert and you buy the marketing rights to sell an intellectual property.

The beauty of royalty income is that the costs for establishing the ownership of a qualifying property are paid in "old money" (i.e., pre-inflation money), while future royalties will increase with inflation.

However, there is a caveat. To offer inflation protection, the royalty contract must link the calculation of future royalty payments to a mutually agreed inflation rate. For example, there is no inflation protection if the owner sells the right to market their intellectual property at a fixed price. In fact, the owner will be exposed to a substantial inflation risk if payments are not linked to future inflation rates.

There are many ways royalty income streams can be generated. If set up correctly, royalties can be an attractive income source.

PATENTS

Patents can offer inflation protection in many different forms. We will focus on two forms.

First, the patent owner markets their invention on their own by selling the patented products or selling marketing licenses to third parties. It is important that licensing fees are explicitly linked to future inflation rates.

Second, a person may buy a patent from the original inventor and start marketing the invention on their own. This option is particularly interesting for experienced sales people.

Obviously, the attractiveness of the patent in terms of generating future sales is an important consideration.

COMMERCIAL SOCIAL MEDIA ACTIVITIES

There are social media outlets that pay for the content that users have published. Some thresholds have to be met, though. A prominent example is the platform YouTube. Under certain conditions (e.g., meeting goals for subscribers and viewing time), the platform pays for the content posted by a user. The remuneration is based on an algorithm that seems to rely on the number and characteristics of viewers.

There is a wide range of content that receives great interest on social media platforms such as YouTube including home repair, academic tutorials, baking, and sports. In short, this option is widely available.

The beauty of this business model is that very few upfront investments are needed to post content on YouTube or other platforms that pay for content. In most cases, a higher-end smartphone is enough to get started. Once a content publication has been uploaded to the respective platform, the author is entitled to future revenue streams without being required to invest additional time or money.

AFFILIATE MARKETING PROGRAMS

Affiliate marketing has become a booming industry. Many companies allow you to promote their products on your social media platforms (e.g., your website) and pay you a commission for each sale that is traced back to you.

Typically, you first sign up with a company or online service as an affiliate. After you have been accepted, you can start marketing the company's products through your website, blog, social media posts, or videos (note: some exclusions and limitations apply). For each sale you will receive a commission.

Although this industry is rapidly evolving and changing, affiliate marketing programs have become an attractive income source for many people.

MEMBERSHIP AND SPONSORSHIP INCOME

Many content providers that have a large followership are considered experts or opinion leaders on certain topics. Sometimes, they are just entertainers who spread interesting ideas or observations.

To generate income, many content providers have created communities on social media that charge a membership or access fee. The topics they cover can range from personal development to specific hobbies. The key is to find a community that is large enough to justify one's efforts.

Paid content can be sold to members in many different forms:

- Newsletters
- Blogs
- A website with different forms of content (e.g., articles, videos, checklists)
- A moderated discussion forum
- Webinars
- Online courses

Once a community has grown in size, additional income opportunities emerge. For example, sponsorships can be sold to companies and organizations. Marketing time can be sold to sell or advertise products and services.

In addition, the organizer of a community can also ask for donations. Standardized software is available for inclusion on social media sites. These software packages collect donations (against a fee) and transfer the money to the owner's bank account.

Creating communities has become a fast-growing business in social media. New remuneration options are being developed constantly.

BECOMING A LANDLORD

Becoming a landlord can create passive income streams. The most traditional form of being a landlord is to own a piece of real estate that is rented to tenants.

However, there are additional ways that might be available to you. You can rent out a room in your house or apartment that you do not need or need only on certain days of the week. You can also rent out your garage if you do not need it. When you go on vacation, you may rent out your house to other families.

If you are living in an area that hosts major events during which hotel capacity is insufficient, you may stay with relatives or friends and rent out your house or apartment to event participants.

Related to this opportunity is renting out property you own. This includes items like your car, tools, or baby furniture. Again, the internet is the platform that may help you find customers for such activities.

In conclusion, there are many ways you can raise additional income during periods of high inflation. The ideas presented in this chapter are meant to kick-start your thinking to find ideas that are suitable for you.[25]

Please remember, it is paramount to start with securing your current job and to have contingency plans should you lose your current employment. When you have created this first line of defense, it is much easier to explore opportunities to supplement your income.

---

[25] Reminder: Always check rules and regulations in your jurisdiction.

CHAPTER 9: INCREASE YOUR PRODUCTIVITY (CORE ACTIVITY #4)

Introductory comments:

For many readers, this chapter will come as a surprise. Why do I need to worry about my productivity during an inflation crisis? The answer is simple. Raising our productivity at work and at home will make us more successful and will free up valuable time. We can use this time to reinvest in both the DVBI program and our personal life (i.e., enjoy more time with family and friends, engage in social activities). We will feel better, be more content, and send more positive messages to others.

In this chapter we will pursue the following two victories:

Victory 1 (short-term inflation focus): *In the short term, we need to free up time to invest in the DVBI program (e.g., to reduce our expenses and increase our overall income). Ideally, we do this by raising our productivity and not by neglecting our family, friends, or hobbies. The goal is to succeed with the DVBI program and maintain our life balance.*

Victory 2 (long-term personal growth): *Highly successful people are almost always highly productive people. They do not waste time. Some of them consider time more important than money (as the Roman Stoic philosopher Seneca did). Lost money you can recover. If you waste time, it is lost permanently. By being highly productive, successful people manage to outperform at work and have enough time left for their family and friends and to devote significant time to their hobbies and to learning new things. They are constantly growing; by expanding their minds and intellectual horizon, they can detect new opportunities before others do. In other words, productive people become self-perpetuating success machines.*

If there is anything magic in life, it is productivity. It explains why some people are constantly stressed while others accomplish more in less time. There is no limit to how much we can accomplish within a given unit of time.

There are many ways to raise our productivity. It all depends on how we approach a task. We can get better at a task through repetition and focus (the "learning curve"). We can use innovative approaches or specialized tools to reduce the time needed for finishing a task. We can ask others for help. In management, we refer to the latter as leverage. Leverage plays an important role in raising our productivity.

Productivity as a concept sounds technical and difficult. However, it is not. Perhaps the best and most impressive example of raising productivity (in this case through leverage) is taken from Mark Twain's book, *The Adventures of Tom Sawyer*. Twain narrates the wonderful story of how Tom Sawyer managed to get his aunt's fence painted in one afternoon by convincing his friends to help him do so. He presents painting the fence (which was originally meant to be a punishment for his bad behavior) as a treat and as a meaningful and important task that can only be handled by a special few. We may ignore this act of manipulation for a moment. The key lesson is: Get others involved and ask for support and you will be amazed how quickly you can raise your productivity to unexpected levels.

As a management consultant, I have conducted countless projects intended to raise a client's productivity. Time and again I was surprised by how much improvement was possible. By using all available levers, we helped the client reach new levels in productivity. It all translated into getting more done with fewer resources. In fact, the theme "achieve more with less" should accompany your thinking no matter what you seek to accomplish in life.

There is no reason why we should not learn from big companies and management consultants. Our lives are filled with inefficiencies, ineffectiveness, and unproductivity. Addressing these issues will free up significant amounts of time that can be reinvested into our Beat Inflation program and will create more happiness and fulfillment in our lives.

Before I share my ideas on how to do this, let us first understand the mechanics of productivity.

Raising productivity means one simple thing: raising the output for every unit of input employed. Input can be time, material resources, or financial resources, all of which are important in our Beat Inflation program.

RAISING THE PRODUCTIVITY OF YOUR TIME

Your time is one of the most important assets you have. As mentioned previously, the Roman philosopher Seneca made one of the most important observations of best-practice time management: Time is more important than wealth (money).[26] If we lose money with an investment, we may regain the loss with a more successful investment later on. When it comes to time, the world is different. Time that has passed is not recoverable. The past hour we spent on a meaningless distraction (e.g., social media) is lost forever; it is a permanent loss. We will never recover this hour again.

Seneca makes a powerful point that should motivate us to be more concerned about how we use our time. Time is the most precious resource we have. In fact, it is the only resource that is limited in our lives.

[26] This thought is so important for people seeking to become more successful in life. Unfortunately, many people disregard Seneca's rule and waste enormous amounts of time. This is the reason I have referred to this thought several times.

Therefore, we need to re-focus our approach to time, particularly during periods of economic hardship.

Our goal should be: no more time wasted on meaningless distractions (e.g., undirected surfing on the internet or social media platforms). Instead, we should spend our time on productive purposes (with undivided focus), with people we value highly (e.g., family, friends) or activities that are meaningful to us (e.g., cherished hobbies).

By doing so, we should obtain the following advantages:

1. We need less time for our daily tasks at work. Hence, we generate extra time that can be reinvested.
2. We increase the quality of output for each unit of time invested through focus and elimination of distractions.
3. We perform at a higher level, which will send positive messages to people in our professional and personal environment.

Being more productive will lead to a boost of energy and self-confidence in our lives, which we need when fighting the inflation dragon.

To achieve the goal of higher time productivity, management consultants use a simple task when working with corporate clients. Before we can improve our time productivity, we need to understand how we have allocated our time in the past. Where did all the time go? What activities were performed? What outputs were achieved?

You can do the same thing in your personal life. Use Chart 33 to track your time usage. The first goal is to create transparency about the use of your time over the course of a day. Doing so helps you understand where you waste time or where you can speed up completion of activities by using better strategies (including leverage).

CHART 33: Time Usage Tracking

TIME	TIME USAGE (TASK)	COMMENT
0.00-5:00		
06:00		
07:00		
08:00		
09:00		
10:00		
11:00		
12:00		
13:00		
14:00		
15:00		
16:00		
17:00		
18:00		
19:00		
20:00		
21:00		
22:00		
23:00		
24:00		

By knowing your time allocation, you can then initiate corrective action.

Fill out the form for a minimum of two weeks. Document the activity and add comments about the value added by the respective activity.

Next, review your data and look for the following patterns:

- Time spent on low-value activities (e.g., social media, low-quality entertainment): These are activities that should be drastically reduced. They are "easy wins" to free up valuable time.
- Time spent on high-value activities (e.g., learning a new skill, a new language): It is sometimes insightful to see the relationship between time spent on low- versus high-value activities. We should always strive to use our time as effectively as possible. What is your ratio? Often, this exercise leads to shocking results. If so, that is a good thing as it indicates a high potential for future improvements.
- Track your progress over time: Ideally, the time wasted on low-value activities should converge to zero. This does not mean that you won't have fun in life. Quite the contrary, as spending time with family and friends or on meaningful hobbies is part of the high value-added category. You just want to avoid "goofing off" on meaningless activities that do not create value or valuable memories.
- Excessive amount of time required to accomplish important tasks due to lack of self-organization: Often, our lack of self-organization steals massive amounts of time from us (e.g., looking for a password that we failed to keep in an organized place for easy retrieval or for a bank statement that was not properly filed). Compare the actual time needed for accomplishing a task with a "best-practice approach."
- Activities that could be simplified by having strict routines in place: Sometimes it helps to do similar activities in a certain time window (e.g., paying all your bills on Friday evenings at 6:00 p.m.).

Next, it is important to raise productivity and value creation for each unit of time used during the day. This task is done not only to avoid wasting time on unproductive activities, but to substitute high-value for low-value activities. The goal is to spend as little time as possible on low-value activities.

Raising your productivity is an important task during periods of high inflation as it can make you more valuable to your employer. Attracting positive attention should increase your bargaining power for future salary increases or new job offers from different companies.

The following list summarizes activities that will increase your time productivity:

- Eliminate/reduce low-value activities as they will not have a positive impact on closing the inflation gap.
- Define a set of skills and capabilities that increase your market value in the job market (and raise your bargaining power with your employer). Ask your employer for time off to take classes in subjects that may help you become more efficient and effective at work. For example:
    - Computer programming
    - Languages
    - Marketing/sales
    - Accounting, finance, and other technical areas
    - Certifications that qualify you for a higher salary or promotion
- Perform high-value activities during commuting or down time (e.g., improve language skills while travelling on a bus or sitting in a doctor's waiting room). Use any block of time available to you in a meaningful way.
- Commit to strict routines to become more efficient.
- Practice a high degree of self-organization to avoid time wasted when looking for misplaced items.

- Silence your phone when you do not need it (notification sounds are a major source of distraction).
- Check your email and phone messages at certain time intervals. Avoid constantly interrupting your work flow (or studying) to check for new messages.
- Avoid any form of distraction.

You will be amazed how much can be accomplished in a week if you are working at a higher level of productivity. You will not only waste less time and substitute high-value activities for low-value ones, but will be recognized as a person who gets things done. Such a perception is priceless and will increase your bargaining power with your employer to obtain future promotions or to find a better paid job at a new employer.

RAISING THE PRODUCTIVITY OF YOUR RESOURCES (ASSETS)

All of us own a multitude of different resources, such as a house, cars, tools, books, furniture, and so on.

In most cases, we are not particularly concerned about the productivity of these assets. However, during periods of high inflation this should change. We can increase the productivity of our assets in many different ways.

In principle, we should review our assets for the following income-generating opportunities:

- Sell it (if we do not use it)
- Donate it for a tax receipt (if we do not use it and cannot sell it)
- Rent it to others for an appropriate fee whenever appropriate (if there is demand)
- Trade it for items we can use

Let me give you a few examples:[27]

- An unused garage could be rented out to a third party.
- Expensive tools could be rented out on an hourly/daily basis.
- A yard sale/garage sale could help sell unused items and raise money. You may join forces with other Beat Inflation team members to attract more interested shoppers. Keep in mind, getting rid of items you do not need is liberating (cleaning or maintaining the items will not be required anymore).
- An extra room in your house could be rented out to a student or adult. Alternatively, a quiet room in your house could be rented out as a daytime office to a professional.
- Your house can be rented out to vacationers when you are travelling.
- Your car can be rented out during periods of idleness.
- Your house/garden can be rented out to film crews, for wedding ceremonies, or other special events.

[27] Laws and regulations vary by country, state, and municipality. Please check applicable laws and regulations or other constraints before engaging in any transaction. Also, please check for liability issues and address them as appropriate. This list is meant to get your thinking started.

These ideas are meant to get you started to think like an entrepreneur. Add your own ideas and implement them if appropriate. Making the most out of your assets will help to close the inflation gap.

RAISING THE PRODUCTIVITY OF YOUR FINANCIAL RESOURCES

The productivity of your financial assets can be increased as well. However, doing so may expose you to additional risks. Therefore, it is important to seek the advice of a qualified financial professional before initiating activities. Also, some activities might require certain licenses or are subject to legal rules and regulations in your jurisdiction.

Here are some basic ideas to get started:

- Shop around for higher interest rates on bank accounts.
- Renegotiate fees for savings and checking accounts.
- Drop credit cards that charge high fees for relatively limited services or add-on inclusions (e.g., free insurance).
- Use credit cards with attractive payback programs and low/zero fees.
- Shop around for best rates when looking for a mortgage or consumer loan. Create a competition among mortgage providers and have them bid against each other.
- Review the productivity of your investments.

CHAPTER 10: CONCLUSION AND OUTLOOK

We have reached the end of this book. I sincerely hope that the DVBI program and the many ideas presented were helpful to you.

It was difficult to write this book as no two readers are alike. You may reside in different countries, have different careers, different family situations, or different life circumstances. I had to take all these issues into consideration.

Therefore, I chose a pyramid structure as my format. We started with a framework, and then moved to core activities, sub-activities, and, finally, to practical ideas. It is important to examine a complex issue like inflation with a structured approach.

Not every activity and idea discussed in this book is relevant or applicable for each reader. However, even those ideas that are not relevant to you will accomplish two objectives: First, you will learn about the thinking that is required during periods of high inflation and second, you will use what you have learned to kick-start your own thinking and come up with your own ideas. This should lead to attractive and promising growth opportunities that will make you a more successful, fulfilled, and happier person.

While inflation is a serious risk, it will pass eventually. Typically, the beginning phase is much tougher than the later phases of an inflation period (unless central bankers and politicians in your country fail to contain inflation). You may see some improvements earlier than you originally thought.

For now, do the best you can do to close the inflation gap. Please reach out to others for help and support. I hope that my readers will form many

Beat Inflation teams around the globe and that these teams will exchange experiences and ideas.

Once inflation has passed, please do not discard this program. If you continue to focus on

- monitoring your expenses,
- optimizing your risk taking,
- increasing your income, and
- raising your productivity,

you will be on a good path for a successful, fulfilled, and happy life.

Adhering to these four core activities will keep you focused and will raise your preparedness for whatever challenge in life comes next. Your resilience will rise and so will your self-confidence.

I would like to thank you for purchasing and reading this book. I wish you all the best for the future.

Become legendary!

Yours,

Dr. Wolfgang Hammes

BONUS SECTION: THE FOUR PHASES INFLATION MANAGEMENT MODEL

In my 2016 book *The Return of High Inflation*, I introduced the Four Phases Inflation Management (FPIM) model. I have used this model successfully in my consulting work with corporate clients and have referred to it several times in this book. The model helps you to understand the dynamic nature of an inflation cycle.

Therefore, I have included here a reprint, taken verbatim, of the original description of the FPIM model. I do so because my experience suggests that this model helps both companies and individuals to better navigate through these volatile times.

Please keep in mind that this is a generic model that describes four typical phases of an inflation cycle. Variations occur in real life. For example, during the 1970s inflation crisis policy mistakes by central bankers and politicians prolonged the period of high inflation. More specifically, the U.S. economy experienced two severe inflation shocks. When most people thought inflation was under control, it reemerged during the late 1970s.

It is also possible that you live in a country that will not reach phase four in terms of a real "normalization." For example, during the 1920s period of hyperinflation in Germany, the old currency ("Reichsmark") did not survive. It had to be replaced by a new currency ("Rentenmark").

Again, the framework has been developed to help you approach inflation in a dynamic way, with each phase presenting different opportunities, challenges, and risks. Consequently, each phase requires different strategic responses.

Again, please keep in mind that the following text was published in 2016, long before today's inflation problem has emerged.

THE TOOL: THE FOUR PHASES INFLATION MANAGEMENT MODEL (FPIM MODEL)[28]

A big mistake people make is to believe that inflation is a one-dimensional, static problem. They believe that a single static strategy will protect against inflation risks, similar to a single immunization shot protecting against the ever-changing flu virus. Such static thinking is dangerous and may lead to severe losses during an inflation cycle.

In my experience, it has been helpful to think about high inflation as a cycle or sequence of different phases. Each phase has its own unique set of challenges and opportunities and therefore needs its own tailor-made strategy. When the inflation cycle moves from one phase to another, your strategy must anticipate this move. Otherwise, you may not be able to deal with the new challenges and opportunities that arise.

During any phase of the inflation cycle, you may be severely punished if you fail to anticipate the necessary strategic requirements. This result occurs regardless of whether you did an excellent job of anticipating previous phases of an inflation cycle. As mentioned earlier, inflation is not forgiving; at any stage of an inflation cycle, your company may fail if you do not anticipate the challenges and risks in your environment. An inflation cycle will not give you time to rest. You and your company will be constantly challenged.

---

[28] The FPIM model has been developed to guide strategic decision making for both businesses and individuals before and during inflation cycles. In this chapter, the tool is described from the perspective of a corporate user. However, it can also be used to guide decision making for individuals and to cross-check personal inflation protection strategies. Numbering of footnotes and charts has been adjusted.

Chart 34 shows the phases of a complete inflation cycle. At first glance, you may think that this concept is too simple for an advanced company or advanced investor. However, you must understand that any change of inflation rates can have brutal consequences if you are not properly prepared. In fact, both rising and falling inflation rates can be equally damaging for unprepared companies.

A successful strategy, therefore, adjusts all relevant activities of a company's value chain to the respective issues posed by each phase of an inflation cycle. This includes financing, accounting, inventory management, procurement, marketing, and production. Each activity of a company's value chain can be subject to severe inflation traps that management must understand and address. Chart 34 depicts an inflation cycle as a five phase system including a phase of no inflation (phase zero). Later in this book, when we talk about developing strategies to cope with inflation, we will drop phase zero and focus exclusively on the four remaining phases. For completeness, however, Chart 34 shows the five phases that modern economies undergo over the course of time. It is important to remind ourselves that even the phase of no significant inflation is a normal and recurring period in the overall cycle of rising and falling inflation rates.

Chart 34: The five generic phases of an inflation cycle

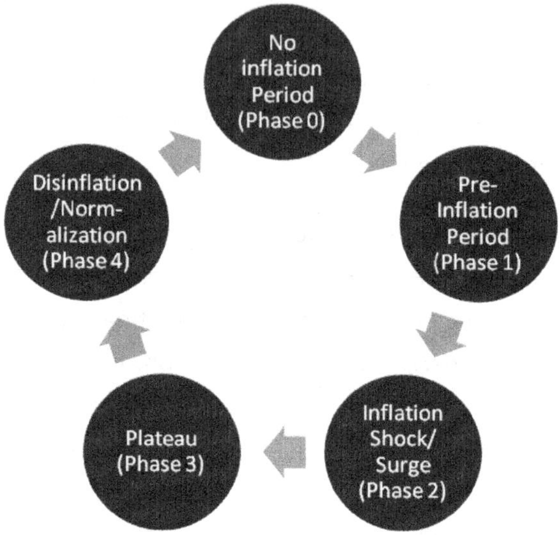

Any inflation cycle starts with phase 0, the period of no visible inflation issues. At that point, few people have inflation risks on their radar screen. Many politicians, central bankers, and managers tend to believe that this phase is infinite and that inflation issues are a thing of the past. This misperception is one of the reasons why inflation will eventually return. Authorities underestimate inflation risks and engage in strategies that will eventually awaken inflation in the future. In paper money systems inflation is never defeated for good. Instead, it is only dormant and will reappear much faster and more viciously than most people can imagine.

The longer an economy or country has been pampered with low inflation rates, the more likely it is that high inflation will eventually (re)appear. For example, the long period of low inflation after World War II might have seduced central bankers in the U.S. (and other countries) to overuse monetary instruments in an attempt to smooth out business cycles and avoid (sometimes healthy) recessions. Practice great caution if pro-inflationary policies are used excessively by central bankers and politicians, particularly after a prolonged period of low inflation rates.

Once a new inflation cycle starts, businesses will not be able to relax for long. Management will be constantly busy and challenged to prepare for the respective phases of an inflation cycle. This includes the period of rising inflation rates (phase 2), the period when inflation rates plateau (phase 3), and eventually the period of falling inflation rates (phase 4). Each phase demands its own strategic responses to protect a company from a rapidly changing business environment. At any phase of an inflation cycle, a company may suffer seriously if it misses crucial turning points in an inflation cycle. The key factor of success is to anticipate these turning points and to implement proper strategic responses at the right time.

A classic example of the challenges of inflation management is the impressive rise and subsequent steep fall of the Stinnes empire during the 1920s hyperinflation cycle in Germany. Hugo Stinnes was one of the most successful German industrialists and entrepreneurs during the 1910s and 1920s. He had an exceptional economic mind and a superb understanding of the mechanics of inflation. Stinnes mastered the first phases of the German hyperinflation cycle extremely well (phases 1–3). He built an industrial empire by basically leveraging debt to acquire a large number of companies and industrial stakes. He repaid his debt later with hugely depreciated money. He knew that using debt was a good inflation hedge, and he was often referred to as the "king of inflation."

Stinnes wisely anticipated the end of the German hyperinflation period and shortly before his death instructed his family to radically reverse his current strategy. He knew that accumulating debt was now a dangerous strategy no longer to be reduced by high inflation. After his death in 1924, his successors ignored his warnings and continued the strategy of debt-based expansion. Soon the Stinnes empire was caught unprepared to deal with the new situation of low economic growth, a new but stable currency, and low inflation. Creditor banks took control and broke up the Stinnes empire.[29]

Many companies and individuals commit similar mistakes when dealing with an inflation cycle. Anyone unprepared to deal with the respective risks and opportunities of each phase of an inflation cycle is likely to be caught unprepared at some time. To avoid this dangerous risk, I have developed a tool that helps keep focus on the crucial four phases of an inflation cycle. This simple tool may be adapted to one's needs and preferences. In some cases, it may make sense to divide one phase into two or more sub-phases to enable a more fine-tuned and surgical response to the challenges of an inflation cycle. For the purpose of this book, let us stick to the four core phases and call the tool the "Four Phases Inflation Management model," or FPIM model (see Chart 35).

---

[29] For a more complete discussion of the inflation strategies employed by Hugo Stinnes and the fate of the Stinnes empire after his death, see Domberg, Rathje (2009): *Die Stinnes – Vom Rhein in die Welt*. The most complete discussion on the life of Hugo Stinnes can be found in Feldman (1998): *Hugo Stinnes*.

Chart 35: The Four Phases Inflation Management model (FPIM model)

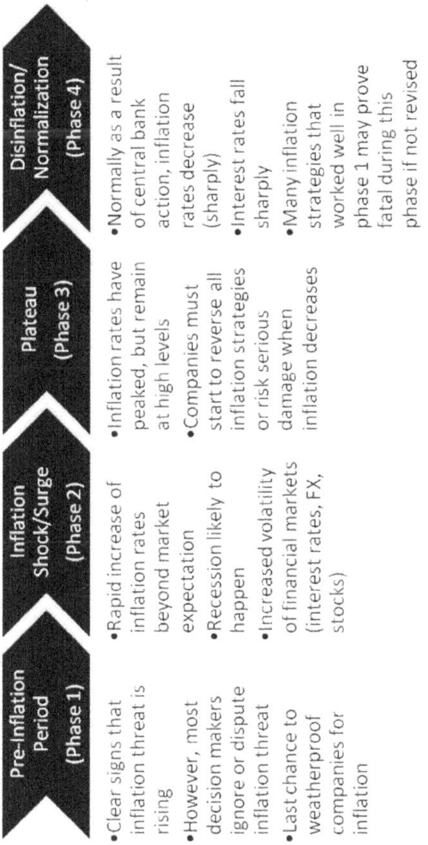

The tool starts in phase 1 of an inflation cycle when authorities implement decisions that will later lead to an acceleration of inflation. Preceding phase 1 is often a long period of low and stable inflation and therefore many people miss detecting these changes in the business environment that will later expose them to significant inflation risks. As I mentioned before, it is important in today's world of fiat paper money systems to view inflation as a recurrent problem, not a singular occurrence of the past. Economies based on fiat money systems should view periods of high inflation as normal occurrences and not as exceptions.

As it may be sometimes difficult for managers to detect early warning signs for an economy moving from phase 0 to phase 1, Chart 36 presents a selection of potential warning signs. It is important to note that the warning signs for EMEG Inflation may be quite different than those for LOFIS Inflation.

Chart 36: Typical phase 1 developments

Typical developments in phase1	Possibly leading to ...	
	EMEG Inflation	LOFIS Inflation
Excessively loose monetary policies	+	++
A central bank that is hyperactive and deeply involved in the economy	+	++
Artificially low interest rates (due to central bank policies)	+	++
Prolonged period of government fiscal deficits	+	++
High absolute and relative levels of government debt	+	++
High levels of (unused) cash in the economy		++
Inflation is not an immediate concern of market participants		+
High debt leverage in the economy (companies, households)		++
Emerging asset bubbles (due to excess liquidity and low interest rates)	+	+
Rising skepticism and doubts regarding politicians and central bankers		++
Limited slack in the economy (unused capacity utilization)	++	
Bargaining power for higher wages is increasing	++	
Signs that demand for commodities, products, and services is starting to outpace supply	++	

It is not uncommon to mistake phase 1 for a time of prosperity and progress. Some developments might actually suggest that the economic situation is improving and risks are diminishing. For example, during the initial phase 1 of the 1970s inflation cycle, U.S. stock markets reached an all-time high (December 1972) and the economy was perceived as being strong. The overall sentiment was characterized by confidence and euphoria about the future. Most companies and individuals failed to see the economic reality in 1972. In 1973, phase 2 of the new inflation cycle started, and it exposed many companies and people to the harsh reality of an inflation-induced recession. Stock markets subsequently lost about half of their value over a twenty-one month period. Needless to say, most companies and people were caught totally unprepared and had to struggle to overcome the enormous challenges presented by a sudden rise of inflation rates.

During phase 2 of an inflation cycle, managers and individuals learn the hard way that the economy and financial markets are more fragile and weak than they previously thought. Unexpectedly, they find themselves in a severe economic storm. That is why we see so many erratic and seemingly irrational decisions during phase 2 of an inflation cycle. Many managers then realize that keeping capital and cash levels low is wrong. They also realize that relying on cheaper short-term variable financing puts them in a difficult spot when interest rates start to rise. Phase 2 is also the time when managers learn the hard way how important long-term procurement contracts for commodities and production materials are in a world of rising prices. With the arrival of phase 2, many established business and management paradigms have to be revised.

Phase 2, however, is not only doom. It presents exceptionally attractive opportunities for those prepared for this situation. At the end of phase 2, investors can purchase stocks and other investment assets at extremely low prices. Companies that did their homework and prepared for the challenges of phase 2 may substantially improve their competitive position, increase market share, or even acquire struggling, undercapitalized competitors at low valuations. The number of companies and individuals who profit from phase 2 of an inflation cycle tends to be low. This is not because it is difficult to exploit the opportunities presented by phase 2, but simply because most people do not do their homework and are not prepared to deal with the risks and opportunities of this phase.

Rising inflation in phase 2 impacts the complete value chain of a company and requires timely strategic and operational readjustments to avoid a dramatic deterioration of profitability. While financing strategies are at the core of safe survival during times of high inflation, they are not the only area of concern. Procurement, pricing, and inventory management issues are also of high importance. The sophisticated CEO may profit from earlier preparation and by understanding how and exactly where high inflation will impact business. Successful CEOs will use the inflation action plan that they diligently prepared before inflation rates started to rise.

In phase 3, inflation remains elevated, but inflation growth rates reach a plateau. It is now crucial to closely monitor central bankers and politicians, who have to make tough decisions that are vastly unpopular (i.e., continue with restrictive monetary policies, stick to conservative fiscal budgets and cut deficits, and commit to structural reforms to kick-start the economy). It takes enormous courage for politicians and central bankers to be determined to end inflation. They have to stick with these harsh policies even if the economy starts to improve and inflation rates start to decrease. If they fail to do so, inflation will rise again and may lapse back into another phase 2 (as it did during the 1970s).

If central bankers and politicians can successfully tame inflation and continue unpopular measures, the inflation cycle moves into the final period: disinflation and normalization (phase 4). Top management needs to reverse current strategies to enable a company to deal with the many consequences of falling inflation. Once phase 4 has started, financing and capital strategies must be revised to account for falling interest rates. Long-term fixed rate loans should be avoided. Falling inflation rates make short-term variable rate loans much more attractive. Equity capital might be available again at more favorable terms than before. Companies that miss this final turning point in an inflation cycle may struggle with high debt costs on long-term financing agreements. The well-financed and strongly capitalized company might find this time attractive for further consolidation efforts, such as acquisitions of business divisions of struggling competitors or takeovers of other companies.

Chart 37 summarizes a selection of important changes that occur in the four critical phases of an inflation cycle.

Chart 37: Changing environments and challenges in the four phases of an inflation cycle (select examples)

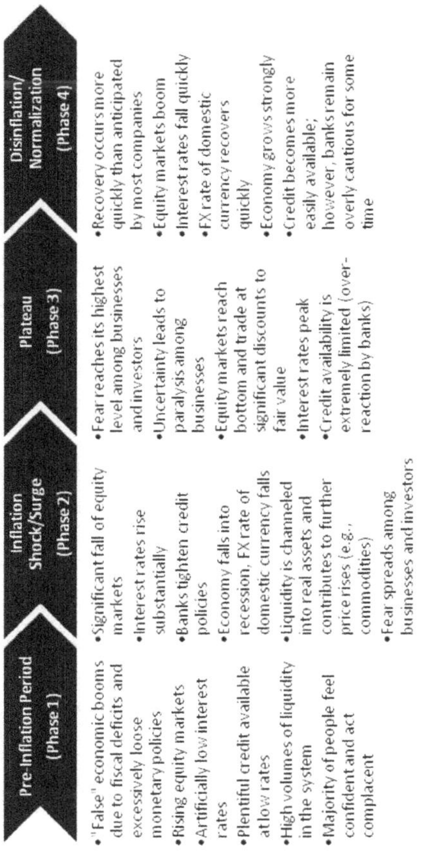

FPIM is a simple and idealistic model of an inflation cycle. Variations from the model are possible and do happen. For example, during the 1970s, we witnessed two inflation shocks (1973–1974 and 1977–1980). Phase 2 occurred twice during that cycle. After the first inflation shock, inflation retreated, but it was not yet beaten. It re-emerged a few years later more aggressively. The reason for this re-emergence of inflation is simple. Central bankers and politicians were not sufficiently committed to implement and uphold the required, but unpopular, policies and reforms necessary to end high inflation. They relaxed monetary policies too early as they felt immense populist pressure due to high unemployment and a weak economy.

Those who anticipated an end to the inflation cycle in 1975 or 1976 were in for a dangerous surprise. After a short retreat, inflation returned during 1977–1980 and reached much higher levels than during the previous inflation shock. It was a repeat of a classic phase 2 of an inflation cycle accompanied by a severe and deep recession.

Beating inflation is like treating a dangerous infection with antibiotics. If patients declare victory over the infection too early and stop the course of treatment too soon, the infection is likely to come back even more viciously. If central bankers and politicians relax too early, inflation might return and create more damage than before (as it did in 1977–1980).

Managers need to assess when a victory over inflation is real and when it is not. This is not as difficult as it sounds. There is a distinct difference in terms of the determinedness and conviction with which Reagan and Volcker successfully fought high inflation in 1980–1982 versus the efforts made by previous administrations in 1975 and 1976. Careful examination should help most managers distinguish between false and real wins over inflation.

Another noteworthy variation from the generic FPIM model is Germany's inflation of the late 1910s and early 1920s. Then, phase 4 proved to be extremely abrupt as a successful currency reform put a sudden end to inflation. In the German hyperinflation cycle, the original currency (German paper mark) proved unable to survive. The government consequently replaced the Mark with the Rentenmark, a collateralized construct that was tremendously successful. Its success surprised many people who thought that the new currency would fail as did the old one.

The German inflation period is an example of an inflation cycle spinning out of control and creating irreparable damage to the economy, currency, financial markets, and society. This period provides a rich learning ground for understanding how to deal with extreme cases of high inflation.

Every industry within an economy has its own set of challenges and opportunities that arise during an inflation cycle. It is important to make inflation strategy as industry specific as possible. In the context of this book, it is not possible to provide a detailed discussion on how inflation impacts different industries. Some aspects regarding the banking and insurance sector are discussed. Based on work with my clients, an industry- and company-specific analysis can help develop efficient and effective strategies capable of reducing most severe inflation risks. They may also enable companies to unlock many opportunities to outwit the competition and to improve a company's strategic positioning.

Across all industries, there are many mistakes companies tend to commit that can result in significant costs and deterioration of competitiveness. Chart 38 lists a selection of typical mistakes. This list is neither complete nor sufficiently detailed. There is a long checklist of issues that I employ when working with clients on this topic. This level of detail, however, would go beyond the scope of this book. The selection of topics presented in Chart 38 enables us to recognize dangerous inflation traps.

Chart 38: A selection of inflation traps over an inflation cycle

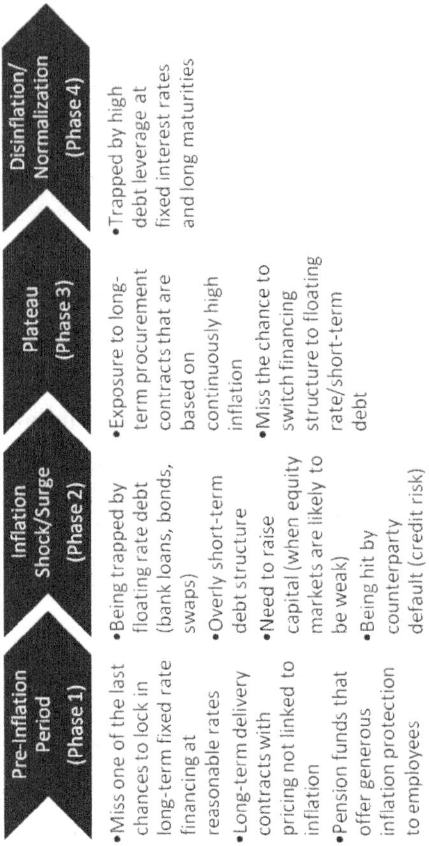

BIBLIOGRAPHY

Domberg, Bernhard-Michael; Rahtje, Klaus: Die Stinnes – Vom Rhein in die Welt, Vienna 2009

Feldman, Gerald: Higo Stinnes, Biographie eines Industriellen 1870-1924, Munich 1998

Hammes, Wolfgang: The Return of High Inflation, Boca Raton 2016

Hammes, Wolfgang: Success through Critical Thinking, Boca Raton 2019

Seneca: Dialogues and Essays – A new translation by John Davie, Oxford 2008

ACKNOWLEDGMENTS

I had the privilege to be educated by many exceptional people. My professional success would not have been possible without the time many different people invested in my education. Therefore, I would like to thank my parents, grandparents, godfather, and other relatives who always encouraged me to focus on education and learning.

Second, I would like to thank my teachers and professors at the following schools: Grundschule Trier-Pallien (Germany), Friedrich-Wilhelm Gymnasium Trier (Germany), Universitaet Trier (Germany), and Clark University (United States). Too often we forget to give thanks for the hard work of our teachers who selflessly spend their lives making their students more successful. The teachers I have known were truly amazing.

Third, I would like to thank all the people with whom I had a chance to discuss the topic of inflation since the publication of *The Return of High Inflation* in 2016. This group includes clients, readers, academics, former colleagues, and friends. Your comments and suggestions are highly appreciated.

Special thanks are due to Diane Adams for the difficult task of editing this book and making it more readable. Additionally, many thanks to my son Maximilian Hammes for proofreading the document.

Finally, I would like to thank my wife, Angela, and our children, Claudia and Maximilian, for their support and encouragement during the writing process.

Let me also thank every reader for spending time with this book. I hope you will gain some valuable insights.

ABOUT THE AUTHOR

Dr. Wolfgang H. Hammes was a partner at the management consultancy firm McKinsey & Company (New York), where he was a leader of the firm's strategic risk management consulting activities and its global financial institutions group. He was a managing director in investment banking for both Merrill (previously Merrill Lynch) and Deutsche Bank AG (London), where he advised leading financial institutions on mergers and acquisitions, capital management strategies, and risk management issues.

Dr. Hammes was one of the first experts who foresaw the financial crisis of 2007-2008. As early as 2000, he warned publicly that a major financial crisis was unavoidable if risk management deficiencies in the financial industry remained unaddressed. He was also one of the first experts who warned about a return of high inflation to the developed world. His 2016 book, *The Return of High Inflation,* correctly predicted the current inflation crisis.

Dr. Hammes is the co-founder and managing director of The Vangi Group LLC, a consultancy boutique specializing in strategic inflation risk management, strategic risk management, and future anticipation.

Dr. Hammes is also the founder and CEO of Hammes Performance Improvement Group LLC, which conducts multidisciplinary research to decode the patterns and factors leading to success and failure. It uses the latest insights from neuroscience, psychology, sociology, philosophy, sports science, business history, and military science to develop strategies, programs, and frameworks to help companies, teams, and individuals become more successful. The company is in the process of launching two major training initiatives: *Unchained Thinking* (a new and more effective way of thinking and organizing cognitive activities) and *From Average to Great* (a program helping individuals exploit their full success potential and become great performers in their chosen "life arenas").

Dr. Hammes has a doctorate degree (summa cum laude) in business administration from Trier University (Germany) and an MBA from Clark University (United States), for which he received a full scholarship from the German government (DAAD). He was a member of the board of trustees at Clark University, where he headed the strategy and finance, compensation, and strategic risk committees.

He has authored four books and has published many articles on strategy, inflation management, success, critical thinking, and risk management topics. He is also an active speaker at international conferences and company events in North America and Europe.

OTHER BOOKS BY THE AUTHOR

The Return of High Inflation: Risks, Myths, and Opportunities **(Boca Raton, 2016)**

Dr. Wolfgang Hammes was one of the first experts who foresaw and warned of a return of high inflation. In this book, Dr. Hammes described why high inflation was a likely outcome of past mistakes in setting monetary and fiscal policies and what to do about it.

The book contains many frameworks, concepts, case examples, and analogies to help structure the reader's thinking, improve understanding of the topic, and support the development of strategic and tactical responses.

The author explains in great detail the likely implications for the economy, society, financial markets, businesses, and individuals. Among others, the book discusses the following important topics:

- Why a return of high inflation could create a perfect storm that will threaten economic stability, disrupt financial markets, and destabilize social and political order.
- Historic case examples of how governments, companies, and individuals have responded to inflation risks, including best- and worst-practice examples. Typical mistakes and pitfalls of failed inflation management strategies are explained.
- A dynamic management tool is presented (The Four Phases Inflation Management model) to guide both companies and individuals in their efforts to manage inflation risks and opportunities through a period of high inflation.
- Why financial institutions are highly vulnerable to inflation risks and why a new financial crisis could be caused by a return of high inflation.

- A detailed case study of the 1970s' inflation crisis (the stagflation period) that includes many lessons learned and a retrospective description of best-practice responses for each phase of an inflation crisis.
- Case examples of people who managed to turn inflation risks into great opportunities (e.g., Warren Buffett, Hugo Stinnes).
- A look into the future, once the current inflation crisis has passed.

Inflation management requires a set of skills different from those taught in today's business schools. This book seeks to close this gap and to enable the reader to craft effective Beat Inflation strategies.

Success through Critical Thinking: Creating a Launchpad to Success **(2019)**

FINALIST: ERIC HOFFER BOOK AWARD

This book is for readers who want to become more successful. How? By teaching a skill that is one of the most powerful success enablers: critical thinking.

The simple truth is that success is not accidental, nor is failure. Both are the consequences of the thinking and analysis that precede decisions and behaviors. Consequently, improving thinking will enable us to make better decisions that lead to more success, happiness, and fulfillment.

Success is the result of superior decisions based on rigorous analysis and thorough understanding. Therefore, long-term success requires complete understanding of critical thinking and the ability to apply it in decision making.

Success through Critical Thinking is a practical study guide presenting powerful concepts, tools, frameworks, and ideas formed from critical thinking. The book not only helps to fully exploit a person's success potential, it also seeks to extend it.

This book seeks to end unfulfilled expectations, underachievement, and failures by teaching, step-by-step, the powerful concepts and tools of critical thinking. Real-life examples taken from business, finance, and sports serve as illustrations. Practice exercises are included at the end of each chapter. The powerful combination of practical teaching, real-life examples, and practice exercises creates a launchpad for achieving more success and better life outcomes. From martial arts, the author adopted the concept of mastering different colored belts (i.e., white belt to brown belt) to mark the progress in the reader's learning.

Particular focus has been given to high practicality, easy implementation, and fast improvements.

Books in preparation:

The Superperformers – Why Winners Win and Losers Lose (planned release date: June 2023)

The book seeks to identify the key factors that explain the achievements of highly successful people. There is good news: The twenty-five lessons learned from analyzing a group of exceptionally successful people can be adopted by everyone seeking to become more successful. Implementing these practices is not rocket science. Advanced degrees from elite universities are not required.

Through my work as an academic, consultant, and investment banker, I have interacted with thousands of people coming from very different backgrounds in terms of nationality, education, culture, and life experiences. This diverse pool of individuals enabled me to compare different life strategies leading to different life outcomes. This pool became the empiric foundation that led to this book.

In this database is a small group of exceptional people who seemed to know the secret principles of success and failure. No matter what they did in life, they always ended up outperforming others and moving to the top of their respective fields. Even when moving to different countries, changing career paths, or switching to different, unfamiliar industries, they quickly rose to the top in their new competitive arena. I call them Superperformers.

These Superperformers became the center of my research in success. The goal was to find common factors and patterns that explained their outperformance vis-à-vis other ambitious and talented people. I started by comparing their strategies and behavioral conduct to that of less successful people. This long and cumbersome process enabled me to derive unique new insights and ideas about performance improvement and success management.

The book describes in detail twenty-five key lessons learned about long-term outperformance. It can be used as a roadmap for those seeking more success, fulfillment, and happiness in life.

Made in the USA
Monee, IL
10 June 2025

19157479R00115